Catechizing with Liturgical Symbols

Twenty-Five Hands-On Sessions
for Teens and Adults

Pamela J. Edwards

Resource Publications, Inc.
San Jose, California

Reprint Department
Resource Publications, Inc.
160 E. Virginia Street #290
San Jose, CA 95112-5876
408-286-8505 (voice)
408-287-8748 (fax)

**Library of Congress
Cataloging in Publication Data**
Edwards, Pamela J., 1953-
    Catechizing with liturgical symbols : twenty-five hands-on sessions for teens and adults / Pamela J. Edwards.
    Includes bibliographical references.
    ISBN 0-89390-401-5
    1. Catholic Church—Liturgy—Study and teaching. 2. Christian art and symbolism—Study and teaching. 3. Christian education of teenagers. 4. Christian education of adults. I. Title.
    BX1970.E27   1997
    264'.02'0071—dc21   95-53162

Printed in the United States of America

01 00 99 98 97 | 5 4 3 2 1

Editorial director: Nick Wagner
Prepress manager: Elizabeth J. Asborno
Production assistants: Mike Sagara,
    David Dunlap

CONTENTS

ACKNOWLEDGMENTS

Profuse and grateful thanks to:

- My editor, Nick Wagner, who handled all my long-distance creative wailing, breast-beating, and gnashing-of-teeth with good-humored aplomb.
- My parents, Harry and Margaret Edwards, who made art and music an integral part of my everyday life.
- Jamie Aven, my "good buddy" through the freelance jungle, whose art graces these pages (Good Shepherd, Mary, and Angel).
- Sister Lou Ella Hickman, IWBS, who skillfully blended the Mysteries of the Rosary and the Beatitudes.
- Karen Dunlap, a faithful companion on the journey.

Thanks also to the copyright holders who granted permission to reprint the following:

- The Scripture quotations contained herein are from the New Revised Standard Version of the Bible, copyrighted, 1989 by the Division of Christian Education of the National Council of the Churches of Christ in the United States of America, and are used by permission. All rights reserved.
- Excerpts from the English translation of *Rite of Baptism for Children* © 1969, International Committee on English in the Liturgy, Inc. (ICEL); excerpts from the English translation of *The Roman Missal* © 1973, ICEL; excerpts from the English translation of *The Liturgy of the Hours* © 1974, ICEL; excerpts from the English translation of *Rite of Penance* © 1974, ICEL; excerpts from the English translation of *A Book of Prayers* © 1982, ICEL; excerpts from the English translation of *Rite of Christian Initiation of Adults* © 1985, ICEL; excerpts from the English translation of *Book of Blessings* © 1988, ICEL. All rights reserved.
- Excerpts adapted from *Catholic Household Blessings and Prayers* © 1988 United States Catholic Conference, Washington, DC; excerpts adapted from the *Book of Blessings* with additional blessings for use in the United States of America © 1988 USCC. Used with permission. All rights reserved. These articles may not be reproduced in any form or by any means without permission in writing from the copyright holder.
- "Our Lady of Guadalupe Prayer" from *Traditional Catholic Prayers* edited by Msgr. Charles Dollen, © 1990, and "On the Song of Songs" from *Bernard of Clairvaux: A Saint's Life in Word and Image* by M. Basil Pennington, OCSO, and Dr. Yael Katzir, © 1994. Permission to reproduce copyrighted materials was extended by Our Sunday Visitor, 200 Noll Plaza, Huntington, IN 46750.
- From "Terry Anderson and Father Martin Jenco: Free to Forgive" by John Bookser Feister (*St. Anthony Messenger* [Dec. 1992]). Reprinted with permission.
- From *The Dialogue* translated by Suzanne Noffke, OP, © 1980 Paulist Press. Used with permission.
- "I Dream of the Rood" in Bernard Mischke, OSC, and Fritz Mischke, OSC, *Pray Today's Gospel* © 1980 Alba House. Used with permission.
- "I Sing a Song of the Saints of God," words by Lesbia Scott; reprinted by permission of Morehouse Publishing.

In the event that some source or copyright holder has been overlooked, please send acknowledgment requirements to the editorial director at Resource Publications, Inc.

INTRODUCTION

You don't have the time. You don't have the money. You can't sew and have never been good at these artsy-craftsy projects, anyway.

These reasons are exactly why you need this book for your ministry. Because whether you work with adults, teens, the catechumenate, environment and art, or you just want to inspire your family prayer-life, you'll find cate-chizing with liturgical symbols immensely enriching. And this book will make it quick and easy for you.

We are a people blessed through our five senses: touch, taste, sight, hearing, and smell. Christ ministered through the five senses of his people to interact with them, to touch them where they were in their faith lives, to galvanize them into conversion and commitment.

So can we. We have the magnificent resources of two thousand years of the Catholic faith on which to draw: Scripture, prayers and liturgies, ritual gestures, symbols, art, the cycle of the liturgical year, music, the words and example of popes, saints, and hardworking laity, and much, much more.

This book offers twenty-five sessions geared toward the liturgical year. Each contains a visual symbol, Scripture or the words of fa-mous Catholics, a mini-prayer liturgy, and instructions on how to make what you need quickly and inexpensively. The sessions are designed to be used in classrooms, on re-treats, for workshops and meetings, and in small spaces. The symbols are meant to be portable, easily and temporarily installed (though we often become sufficiently at-tached to a design and leave it up for several weeks). The sessions can be adapted for large or small groups.

Please don't regard these sessions as cast in stone. Modify them to the needs of your parish or ministry. If you prefer a different prayer text or song or want to add candles where no candles are indicated, adapt. Use these sessions as the basis for your own God-given creativity.

Also, if you don't have all the necessary skills, tap into the gifts of your family, friends, and parish. When some of my co-workers needed real South Texas palms for a Lenten youth retreat, they had their husbands shinny up palm trees with machetes. When I needed a wooden crozier for my Good Shepherd and Pentecost exercises, my friends Keith and Pauline Foegelle kindly provided their wood-working skills to create a marvelous shep-herd's staff from a simple plank of wood.

Environment and Art Tips for the Neophyte

If you have been the Catholic Environment and Art expert at St. Swithins-in-the-Swamp since Vatican II, you can skip this part. But if you flunked Blue Birds (like I did), can't sew a stitch (like I can't), and plan to whip up a lot of these exercises, the following suggestions will help you complete your projects at warp-speed. Please keep in mind that the following items can be collected over a long period of time. Much of it can be looted from your kitchen or garage. It is not necessary to have it all immediately and at once! This is the ideal for which to aim if you really enjoy environ-ment and art.

1. Get plenty of "toys" with which to play.

A generous stockpile of fabric, craft materials, and symbols will electrify the most lackadaisical parish minister, male or female. (Humans are constitutionally incapable of standing idly by while a hands-on project is being constructed. They can do it so much better themselves!)

When I first embarked on Catholic Environment and Art (hereafter referred to as E/A), I painstakingly measured, diagramed, and calculated each project. Now my co-creators and I open my treasure chest of goodies and start throwing together without so much as a sketch. Then we tour each other's creations and compliment each other on our cleverness. That's creativity at its most spontaneous level.

Collect "toys" by cruising craft stores and fabric discount stores. Always keep an eye peeled for sales!

Look for fabric remnants, ribbons, yarns of all colors and textures (burlap, lace, cotton, silk, satin, felt, everything imaginable). Solids in the liturgical colors are most useful, unless you find a pattern that has a symbolic meaning. For example, when I found a remnant of blue cotton cloth dotted with gold stars, I immediately envisioned it as a backdrop for an image of the Virgin Mary.

Keep an eye out for silk flowers, garlands, greenery, wreaths of grapevine, straw, and artificial greens.

Vessels and containers of glass and pottery are useful, and so are candlesticks made of wood, ceramic, or glass.

Rule of thumb: Stay away from plastic!

Symbolic objects: An inexpensive pottery bowl can be used for a washing of the feet rite. A simple cross made from two tree limbs lashed together can move people emotionally. A homemade shepherd's cross can

symbolize a bishop's crozier, Christ as the Good Shepherd, or apostolic ministry. A Bible, of course, is fundamental.

Other suggested items include:

- candles and matches
- inexpensive poster board and stuff to color it (felt-tip pens, paints, colored pencils, or whatever you prefer to work with)
- liturgical calendar, preferably the kind with the colors of the seasons printed on the page

2. Collect tools of the trade.

Once you've got your materials and are panting to put your creative idea into action, you'll need something to put your symbol up. Environment and art advocates wage a constant battle against gravity.

I use one of those plastic household buckets to keep all my tools and widgets in one place. They make it easy to transport supplies from the house, to the car, to the church, and back again.

Recommended stuff to keep in your tool kit:

- Elmer's glue
- scissors (I keep a good pair to cut cloth and a bad pair to cut cardboard, tough rope, sticky tape, etc.)
- glue gun and glue sticks
- string, dental floss, fishing line, florist's wire, twist-ties
- basic tools: hammer, pliers, wire cutters, needle-nose pliers, tweezers, screwdrivers
- sticky tape (all kinds)
- stapler
- measuring tape
- extension cords
- pins (regular pins, silk pins, corsage pins)
- thumbtacks, push pins, safety pins, paper clips
- nails (all sizes)
- rubberbands

- matches
- small sewing kit
- a travel iron that can be used on site before putting up fabric can really make a difference (ideal but an investment)

- small hand hacksaw
- sewing machine (or a good buddy who sews)

Catechizing with Liturgical Symbols

1. OUR LADY, STAR OF THE SEA

Season or Occasion

- any Marian occasion

Purpose

- to seek Mary's guidance and protection through her name "Star of the Sea"

Symbol

The symbol is an image of the Virgin Mary and Baby Jesus with an image of a ship and star attached to signify how Mary helps guide us on our journey to salvation.

Materials

- blue cloth background
- image of Mary with small ship
- stars cut from gold paper
- pins, tacks, or tape to attach stars to cloth

Introduction

The sailing ship as a symbol of the pilgrim church steering toward salvation goes back to the early church. Its image can be found in the ancient catacombs of the underground church in Rome. One of the oldest titles of Mary is Our Lady, Star of the Sea, beloved of mariners on the uncertain ocean. St. Jerome refers to Mary as that part of the sea which is God, and St. Thomas Aquinas sums up her guiding role: "She is called the Star of the Sea because as mariners are guided to their port by the polar star, which is the star of the sea, so also are Christians guided by Mary in the voyage to eternal glory" (Nugent 1). Images of Our Lady, Star of the Sea, show her poised above the ocean waves, glittering with stars or bearing a ship in her hands.

This exercise may be used during appropriate times of the liturgical calendar—in May or October or for other Marian feasts. It is also useful for times of transition, change, decision-making, and uncertainty. It reminds us that although our path may be in doubt, we can always steer a course by Jesus and his Mother. This exercise is also helpful for catechumens who have trouble understanding the role of Mary in Catholicism.

Exercises

1. Read and/or distribute the following text to all participants:

   If you feel yourself tossed by the tempests of the world, turn not away your eyes from the Star of the Sea, if you would avoid shipwreck. If the winds of temptation blow, if sufferings rise up like rocks before you, a look at the star, a sigh towards Mary! If the waves of pride, ambition, calumny, and jealousy seek to swallow up your soul, a look toward the star, a prayer to Mary! If anger, avarice, and love of pleasure splintered your frail boat, seek the eyes of Mary! If horror of your sins, trouble of conscience, and dread of judgments of God begin to plunge you into the gulf of sadness, the abyss of despair, attach your heart to Mary! In your dangers, your anguish, and your doubts, think of Mary, call on Mary! (St. Bernard, as quoted in Nugent 22).

2. Discuss how our parents guided and encouraged us while we were growing up.

   (If this kind of relationship was lacking, discuss what qualities we would have liked present during our childhood and teen years.)

   - As adults, to whom do we offer loving guidance and encouragement and in what form?

   Look up John 19:25-27 and discuss how Christ gave Mary to us as our divine Mother from the Cross.

   - How does Mary offer "parental help" in our daily and spiritual life?
   - What devotional exercises help us to be closer to our divine Mother?

3. Have each one draw and cut out a star from gold paper. Think of a special problem in life that the participant wishes guidance for. Write it on the back, along with a particular attribute of Mary that could help (her loyalty, her love, her compassion for those who admit their guilt and remorse, etc.).

Rite: Our Lady, Star of the Sea

LEADER:

In the name of the Father, and of the Son, and of the Holy Spirit.

ALL:

Amen.

LEADER:

From its earliest years, the church has looked to Mary, the Mother of God, for guidance and protection. The oldest intercessory prayer to Mary dates back to the fourth century:

> We turn to you for protection,
> holy Mother of God.
> Listen to our prayers
> and helps us in our needs.
> Save us from every danger,
> glorious and blessed Virgin
> ("Sub Tuum Praesidum,"
> A Book of Prayers).

Let us place ourselves under the care of our divine Mother by reciting St. Bernard's prayer, the "Memorare" (from A Book of Prayers):

ALL:

> Remember, most loving
>   Virgin Mary,
> never was it heard
> that anyone who turned to you
>   for help
> was left unaided.

> Inspired by this confidence,
> though burdened by my sins,
> I run to your protection
> for you are my mother.

> Mother of the Word of God,
> do not despise my words

> of pleading
> but be merciful and hear my prayer.
> Amen.

LEADER:

(Direct each participant to walk forward and pin the star on the blue cloth background behind the image of Mary while all recite the "Litany of Loreto" (abbreviated, from A Book of Prayers).)

ALL:

> Lord, have mercy
> Christ have mercy
> Lord, have mercy

> God our Father in heaven,
>   have mercy on us
> God the Son, Redeemer of
>   the world, have mercy on us
> God the Holy Spirit, have mercy
>   on us

> Holy Mary, pray for us
> Holy Mother of God, pray for us
> Most honored of virgins, pray for us

> Mother of Christ, pray for us
> Mother of divine grace, pray for us
> Mother most pure, pray for us
> Mother of good counsel, pray for us
> Mother of our Savior, pray for us
> Virgin most wise, pray for us
> Virgin rightly renowned, pray for us
> Virgin gentle in mercy, pray for us
> Faithful Virgin, pray for us
> Mirror of justice, pray for us
> Throne of wisdom, pray for us
> Cause of our joy, pray for us

> Vessel of selfless devotion,
>   pray for us
> Mystical Rose, pray for us

Tower of David, pray for us
Tower of ivory, pray for us
House of gold, pray for us
Ark of the covenant, pray for us
Gate of heaven, pray for us
Morning Star, pray for us
Health of the sick, pray for us
Refuge of sinners, pray for us
Comfort of the troubled, pray for us
Help of Christians, pray for us

Queen of angels, pray for us
Queen of patriarchs and prophets,
    pray for us
Queen of apostles and martyrs,
    pray for us
Queen of confessors and virgins,
    pray for us
Queen of all saints, pray for us
Queen conceived in grace,
    pray for us
Queen of the rosary, pray for us
Queen of peace, pray for us

Lamb of God, you take away
    the sins of the world,
    have mercy on us
Lamb of God, you take away
    the sins of the world,
    have mercy on us
Lamb of God, you take away
    the sins of the world,
    have mercy on us

LEADER:
Pray for us, O Holy Mother of God.

ALL:
That we may be made worthy of the
promises of Christ.

LEADER:
Let us pray. We beseech Thee, O Lord
God, grant that thy servants enjoy
perpetual health of mind and body, that
through the glorious intercession of
blessed Mary ever Virgin, we may be
delivered from present glory and enjoy
everlasting happiness. Through Christ our
Lord.

ALL:
Amen.

LEADER:
In conclusion, let us put our problems in
the hands of Mary and trust in her
guidance as St. Bernard did when he
wrote,

> Let Mary be on your lips, in your
> heart....Following her, you cannot
> wander; while you pray for her,
> you cannot be without hope; as
> long as you think of her, you will be
> in the path; you cannot fall when
> she sustains you; you have
> nothing to fear while she protects
> you; if she favors the voyage, you
> will reach safety's harbor without
> weariness (quoted in Nugent 22).

ALL:
(Sing "Immaculate Mary" or other
appropriate Marian hymn.)

2. PRAYING THE ROSARY/BEATITUDES

Season or Occasion

- any Marian occasion
- catechumenate instruction on how to pray the rosary

Purpose

- to match the Beatitudes with the mysteries of the rosary and thereby more deeply explore the meaning of Mary's faith journey as the Mother of God

Symbol

The symbol used in this session is a large wall-rosary made from silk roses, artificial vine, and a crucifix. Since expense prohibits making the usual number of "beads" out of silk roses,

I've abbreviated this rosary. It consists of five roses for each mystery plus the roses needed just above the crucifix for the Our Father, the three Hail Marys, and the Glory Be. Instead of an Our Father "bead" to connect each set of mysteries, I used a circlet of artificial vine.

Materials

- twenty red silk roses
- one length of artificial vine
- one crucifix
- twist ties or florist's wire
- one large "Christ candle" (optional)
- candles for participants (optional)
- a souvenir silk rose for each participant (optional)

Introduction

As the rite in this session, written by Sr. Lou Ella Hickman, IWBS, says, "Jesus tell us, 'Yearn/Learn to see God.'" Jesus' Sermon on the Mount suggested how we may do that. In the Beatitudes, Christ taught that money, power, and prestige are not the way to see God; rather, those who are merciful, peacemakers, persecuted, and pure of heart will draw closer to God.

The rite also says, "It isn't easy for an adult to become...touchable, teachable, and vulnerable." One of the most touchable, teachable, and vulnerable people in salvation history was Mary, the Mother of God. Through her life, the Beatitudes were made flesh.

Listening to sacred stories encourages us to strip off our own worldly armor and become open to God. We may be inspired by the "beatific" story of Mary as told through the mysteries of the rosary. A woman of little social standing, Mary willingly yielded to the mystery of God's plan for salvation—though it meant poverty, insecurity, and suffering. She lived what we are called to do.

The Beatitudes were addressed to the *anawim* of Christ's time: people poor in material wealth, yearning for the spiritual blessings promised by God. In contradiction to the religious belief of the time (which held that poverty and suffering were punishment for personal sin) Jesus taught that God blesses the poor and powerless who seek his kingdom.

This exercise shows us how God not only gave us the Son but also gave us Jesus' Mother as an example of the way to salvation.

Exercise

1. Reflect on and/or discuss the times we have failed to be "Beatitude people."

2. Choose one aspect of the Beatitudes you wish to act on: make peace, be more merciful, etc. Write it on a piece of paper and tie it with ribbon to make a scroll. Slip a silk rose under the ribbon. Hold the scroll during the rite and keep it as a souvenir.

Rite: Praying the Rosary/Beatitudes

(The idea of matching the Beatitudes with the mysteries of the rosary and the text of this rite are used courtesy of Sr. Lou Ella Hickman, IWBS.)

Pray the rosary using the symbol wall-rosary. The use of candles and multiple speakers can make praying this rosary more exciting. If your group is large enough, different participants can light a candle from a central "Christ candle" as each silk rose "Hail Mary" is said. (The number of Hail Marys usually said during a rosary is reduced here, but a full rosary may be said.) Different people may read the commentaries in the rite and lead the "Hail Marys" and other prayers.

The first reading given refers to each Mystery, and the second reading links each Mystery to a Beatitude.

LEADER:
In the name of the Father, and of the Son, and of the Holy Spirit.

ALL:
Amen.

LEADER:
In his Sermon on the Mount, Christ spoke to the *anawim* of Israel—people poor in material goods, yearning for the spiritual blessings of God. Contrary to the belief of his time that wealth meant God's favor, Christ taught that the poor, the oppressed, the merciful, and the peacemakers were loved by God. In the life of Mary, the Mother of God, the Beatitudes were made flesh. She willingly yielded to God's plan for salvation—even though it meant poverty, insecurity, and suffering. Mary lived what we are called to do. Let us pray that through Mary's example, we may embrace the Beatitudes in our own lives.

(Begin the rosary by saying the Apostle's Creed, the Our Father, three Hail Marys, and the Glory Be.)

READER:
The Joyful Mysteries.

ALL:
Our Father....

READER 1:
The Annunciation
(read Lk 1:26-38; Mt 5:3-4).

This is when it all begins—when Mary allows God into her life. Her life will be a total commitment to the reign of God. Joy can come after I've felt the sadness of not listening to God's love.

ALL:
(Say the Hail Mary and the Glory Be.)

READER 2:
The Visitation
(read Lk 1:39-56; Mt 5:5-6).

Mary was truly filled because she was empty of self. But that was only the beginning. "She went in haste," Luke writes—she was eager to share her great secret with another who had an accepting heart. Elizabeth was amazed—"Who am I that the mother of my Lord should come to me?" she exclaimed.

Who am I that God should love me so?

ALL:
(Say the Hail Mary and the Glory Be.)

READER 3:
The Birth of Jesus
(read Lk 2:1-7; Mt 5:7-8).

Imagine—mercy is a baby! But it isn't easy being born; it's painful and scary. It isn't easy for an adult to become a little child—to become touchable, teachable, and vulnerable. That's the great thing about children—how they love to be touched, how they love to learn, and how easily they can be hurt. The prophet Isaiah wrote, "Learn to do good." Jesus tells us, "Yearn/Learn to see God." What joy!

ALL:
(*Say the Hail Mary and the Glory Be.*)

READER 4:
Presentation of the Child Jesus
in the Temple
(*read Lk 2:22-24; Mt 5:9-10*).

Jesus, Son of God, the Father's greatest gift, is returned. Instead of making peace, this gift will be the sharpest of swords, even wounding his own mother. Joy without sorrow can be shallow entertainment—momentary, fleeting. Sorrow without joy and the laughter in gift-giving becomes despair.

ALL:
(*Say the Hail Mary and the Glory Be.*)

READER 5:
Finding the Child Jesus in the Temple
(*read Lk 2:41-52; Mt 5:11-12*).

Sometimes it's hard when others close to you cannot fathom what you do. Other times it's hard enough to understand—much less accept—what you do yourself. Either way, persecution from others would be so much easier because then I wouldn't have to struggle with self-acceptance.

Jesus, you told your parents what you needed to say. Funny, they didn't understand, and they were already about the Father's business. You said something

about that once: "Lord, when did we not see you and attend to you in your need?"

READER:
The Sorrowful Mysteries.

ALL:
Our Father....

READER 1:
The Agony in the Garden
(*read Lk 22:39-46; Mt 5:3-4*).

St. Paul wrote: "For our sake [God] made him to be sin who knew no sin, so that in [Christ] we might become the righteousness of God" (2 Cor 5:21). How can God's reign be found in such loneliness and sorrow? Jesus experienced the abyss of being separated from the Father. People often speak of hell on earth—well, this is it. Jesus experienced it and he sweated blood over it. For him to say yes to the Father was not automatic. It was a struggle. The devil who tempted him in the desert came back, "Don't suffer; don't die. And if you do, you'll die a failure."

ALL:
(*Say Hail Mary and the Glory Be.*)

READER 2:
The Scourging at the Pillar
(*read Lk 27:24-26; Mt 5:5-6*).

I want to help—I want to fix things for those I love. It would be so much easier to bear if I were the one in distress rather than someone else. But having my hands tied and not being in control—maybe that's what it takes for me to discover exactly how much I really want to be holy. Truly I must hunger for God and not for what God can do for me.

ALL:
(*Say the Hail Mary and the Glory Be.*)

READER 3:
The Crowning with Thorns
(read Mk 15:16-20; Mt 5:7-8).

This is the face of mercy: weariness, dressed in a soldier's old coat. Everything is a blur.

My mercy is like that: a blur, unsure, uncertain, divided. Lord, your mercy is single-hearted: complete, sufficient, total.

ALL:
(Say the Hail Mary and the Glory Be.)

READER 4:
Carrying the Cross
(read Lk 23:26; Mt 5:9-10).

There are people who make peace to avoid conflict. Peace at any price is not peace at all—only delayed warfare. The peace of the cross is truth. This truth is the embrace of conflict—over and over again. In facing conflict, I embrace the cross. Also, in facing the difficult, hidden parts of myself, I learn to accept the reign of God.

ALL:
(Say the Hail Mary and the Glory Be.)

READER 5:
The Crucifixion
(read Lk 23:32-38; Mt 5:11-12).

It is finished!

ALL:
(Say the Hail Mary and the Glory Be.)

READER:
The Glorious Mysteries

ALL:
Our Father....

READER 1:
The Resurrection
(read Mt 28:1-6; 5:3-4).

You spoke Mary Magdalene's name when she cried as she looked for you in the garden. But have I ever really heard you call me by name?

Have I really listened?

Do I take time to listen?

Do I hear you in daily events? Other people?

Do I listen to myself?

How many times have I missed you calling my name?

ALL:
(Say the Hail Mary and the Glory Be.)

READER 2:
The Ascension
(read Lk 24:50-53; Mt 5:5-6).

My hunger for God can die like anything else. This hunger is what makes me the human being that I am. Jesus died before he let his passion for the Father's will die. Now he goes back to the Father so he will be present to us also—forever.

ALL:
(Say the Hail Mary and the Glory Be.)

READER 3:
The Descent of the Holy Spirit
(read Acts 2:1-4; Mt 5:7-8).

The experience of the Spirit is the surprise that God does and will use me. In a world that has forgotten sin, I, too, have forgotten. God respects and honors my struggle. He asks no more than this struggle. In so doing, God uses me for God's glory.

ALL:
(Say the Hail Mary and the Glory Be).

READER 4:
The Assumption
(read Rev 12:1; Mt 5:9-10).

In Mary, I see what it means to be a Christian, what the church can be, and what the reign of God must be like. Mary doesn't give advice to Jesus' followers. And Mary, too, waited on the Lord like everyone else. She is just present—open to God's gift of Godself. That is peacemaking—in the truest sense.

ALL:
(Say the Hail Mary and the Glory Be).

READER 5:
Mary Is Crowned Queen of Heaven and Earth
(read Rev 21:6-7; Mt 5:11-12).

It's hard not to go along with the crowd. It's hard not to worry about what other people think. Yes, it is very hard to do what is right. It is also very hard to keep doing what is right and not get discouraged. Doing right or wrong tells us

who we are: blessed even when we don't feel blessed.

ALL:
(Say the Hail Mary and the Glory Be, then:)

> Hail, Holy Queen, Mother of mercy;
> hail, our life, our sweetness,
>   and our hope.
> To you we cry, the children of Eve;
> to you we send up our sighs,
> mourning and weeping in this land
>   of exile.
> Turn, then, most gracious
>   advocate,
> your eyes of mercy toward us;
> lead us home at last
> and show us the blessed fruit
>   of your womb, Jesus.
> O clement, O loving, O sweet
>   Virgin Mary!

(Conclude by singing an appropriate Marian hymn or song based on the Beatitudes.)

3. SORROWFUL MOTHER/GRIEF

Season or Occasion

- Lent and Holy Week
- Feast of Our Lady of Sorrows, September 15
- any occasion of sorrow

Purpose

- to assist in healing pain or grief by spiritually uniting with Our Lady of Sorrows

Symbol

Two symbols are created for this exercise. The theme of symbol #1 (shown at left) is sorrow. A heart cracked with pain is pierced by a sword, symbols of Christ crucified and Mary's sword-pierced heart. On either side are supplicating hands with palms scored by crosses. Above hangs a crown of thorns representing Christ's crucifixion, which Mary shared, which we all share at some point. A bowl receives the "pain scrolls" of the participants.

The theme of symbol #2 (shown at right) is the conclusion of sorrow—healing, new life, and resurrection. The helpless hands now protectively support the heart. Both are healed. Above hangs a victory crown made of vines (living or artificial) and roses, symbol of Mary, and a rising sun of resurrection. A bowl of roses and scrolls printed with "The Memorare" is placed beneath this symbol.

Materials

- felt: red, purple, flesh-colored, green, blue, yellow
- posterboard (sword)
- crown of thorns
- burlap (backdrop, tablecloth)
- gold lamé (backdrop, tablecloth)
- paper (scrolls)
- rope or ribbon (scroll ties)
- silk rose wreath
- roses

Introduction

A woman whose child had died asked her pastor what she could do to help endure the grief. He recommended counseling, the support of family and friends, prayer, sharing her feelings with those suffering a similar loss, proper exercise and diet, etc.—things the woman expected to hear. Then he said: "Hold the image of the Sorrowful Mother in your mind. Even if you can't pray, hold on to that image. She understands your pain. She suffered it too."

September 15 is the Feast of Our Lady of Sorrows. Traditionally, the Seven Sorrows meditations allowed Catholics to spiritually unite with Mary in her grief over the tragic periods in Christ's life. The Scripture-based Seven Dolors of Mary (as they were called) are the basis for a rosary and a chaplet. In the seventeenth century, this devotion was popularly promoted by the Order of Servants of Mary (the Servites).

These prayer-exercises adapt the traditional Seven Sorrows of Mary plus texts from the Feast of the Sorrowing Mother and other familiar Marian prayers. Participants present their own personal sorrows to the blessed Mother and feel her sympathetic presence and protection. As the lay writer, Caryll Houselander, wrote: "Every trifling thing is told to her and every great sorrow; she is the sharer of all earth's joys and griefs. She knew...that the greatest of all griefs is to be unable to mitigate the suffering of one whom we love. But she was willing to suffer that, because that was what He asked of her" (quoted in Nugent 39).

Historically, Mary was depicted by artists as sheltering people of all ages and walks of life under her cloak. As Archbishop Fulton J. Sheen explained: "The nature of her role is not to call her Son's attention to some need, in an emergency unnoticed by Him, nor is it to 'win' a difficult consent. Rather, it is to unite herself to His compassionate mercy and give a human voice to His infinite love. The main ministry of Mary is to incline men's hearts to obedience to the will of her Divine Son" (quoted in Nugent 6).

Exercises

1. Write any pain or grief you are suffering (or the suffering of someone you know) on a piece of paper, placing it under Mary's protection. Roll the paper up and tie it with a piece of rough twine or hemp rope. This will be offered to Mary during this session's rite.

2. Show participants both wall-symbols and discuss their meanings.

- Do the symbols "speak" to the participants' personal feelings and experience?

Rite: Sorrowful Mother/Grief

(Focus first on symbol #1, the Heart Pierced by a Sword. Place symbol #2 a good distance from symbol #1, but keep it conveniently accessible.)

LEADER:
Lord, show us your mercy and love.

ALL:
And grant us your salvation.

LEADER:
Lord, save your people.

ALL:
Lord, make haste to help us.

LEADER:
In the name of the Father, and of the Son, and of the Holy Spirit.

ALL:
Amen.

(Read together:)

> We turn to you for protection,
> holy Mother of God.
> Listen to our prayers
> and helps us in our needs.
> Save us from every danger,
> glorious and blessed Virgin
> ("Sub Tuum Praesidum,"
> *A Book of Prayers*).

ALL:
Save me, O Lord, in your steadfast love.

LEADER:
(Read Ps 31:2-6,15-16,20.)

ALL:
(Repeat the psalm refrain between verses.)

LEADER:
These are the Seven Sorrows of Mary. Let us unite ourselves in spirit with the grief of the Mother of God.

The First Sorrow: Mary hears the prophecy of Simeon (Lk 2:22-35).

While still a very young mother, Mary learned that her son would play a unique role in the salvation of his people. Every mother worries when she thinks of her child out in the world alone, no longer under her protection. Mary must have often pondered how to trust in God's promises when faced with an unknown future.

The Second Sorrow: The flight to Egypt (Mt 2:1-2,7-15).

Though they had committed no crime, Mary, Joseph, and Jesus were forced to leave their home and hide in Egypt. As a refugee, Mary was no stranger to the threat of violence. She knew the loss of home, family, and friends. Often she had no roof over her head, no bed to sleep in. Would Joseph find employment in a strange place? Yet she and Joseph learned how to become a family with Jesus, even when everything else was lost to them.

The Third Sorrow: Jesus is lost in the Temple (Lk 2:41-51).

A family trip is exciting, especially a pilgrimage to a big city like Jerusalem. Mary enjoyed the exhilaration of breaking routine, getting away from daily chores, and seeing the sights with Joseph, Jesus, and their friends. Yet Mary and Joseph also knew the fear of losing their child in a strange place filled with unknown terrors.

They suffered three terrible days, their minds filled with anguished images, until they found Jesus, safe in the Temple. Of course, they reprimanded him! Hadn't he known they were worried? Hadn't they raised him to be more responsible, more considerate? And Jesus didn't even apologize for upsetting them!

The Fourth Sorrow: Mary meets Jesus carrying his cross (Jn 19:12-17).

Mary must have been tremendously proud of her son. He was a good carpenter and provider. His work was respected. He was renowned as a teacher, preacher, and healer. Crowds followed him wherever he went.

Now she saw the son she loved publicly humiliated, stripped of every shred of dignity. She saw him tried, convicted, and flogged. Her pain was not only for herself but for her son. His pride was shattered, his cause disgraced, his followers vanished. Where were the people who had called him "friend"?

The Fifth Sorrow: Crucifixion (Jn 19:18-30).

The worst had happened to her child. The fears that haunt every mother had come true for Mary. Every disturbing, mysterious prophecy had come to pass. Her son was being executed as a public criminal. They had been abandoned— except for a very few faithful friends.

The Sixth Sorrow: Mary receives Jesus' body from the cross (Jn 19:31-38).

Denied even the faint comfort of the public Jewish mourning ritual, the body of Mary's son was stealthily removed and hidden away. Now she must leave the son she loved in the cold, damp tomb, a tomb that was charity from an outsider. Christ alone.

Mary alone. All their hopes for the future extinguished.

The Seventh Sorrow: Jesus is laid in the tomb (Jn 19:39-42).

Mary had lost her husband and now her only child. Did she feel her life was over? What was her reason for existence? Were the promises of God all lies, all a joke? What was left for her to hold on to?

We have heard the pain that Mary suffered in her life as Mother of God. Yet she knew the resurrection. She found that God's promises come true. So we trust in resurrection in our lives. We trust that she hears our pain as well. Mary will cherish and protect us. For as St. Peter Damian wrote: "Having confidence in you, O Mother of God, I shall be saved; being under your protection, I shall fear nothing; with your help, I shall give battle to my enemies and put them to flight; for devotion to you is an arm of salvation."

Let us offer our prayers and special intentions to the Blessed Mother at this time. Our response will be: "Christ of love, Mother of compassion, hear our prayer."

(Read previously written intentions and invite participants to offer spontaneous intentions as well. During the intercessions, let each participant walk forward and place his or her "pain scroll" under symbol #1, the image of the Sorrowing Mother. Each receives a "Memorare" scroll and a rose from under symbol #2, the resurrection symbol, and returns to his or her seat. LEADER *may wish to play soft instrumental music as background.)*

Let us open our scrolls and read the prayer of St. Bernard entitled "The Memorare" (*A Book of Prayers*). It places our needs in the protective hands of Mary,

who understands and watches over all
our sorrows. Just as she knew healing
and new life, so will we, through her son,
Christ our Lord.

Remember, most loving
    Virgin Mary,
never was it heard
that anyone who turned to you
    for help
was left unaided.

Inspired by this confidence,
though burdened by my sins,

I run to your protection
for you are my mother.

Mother of the Word of God,
do not despise my words
    of pleading
but be merciful and hear my prayer.
Amen.

ALL:
(*Sing a Marian hymn appropriate for the
occasion and season.*)

4. EPIPHANY

Season or Occasion

- Epiphany

Purpose

- to experience the creation of "sacred space" within a ministry environment
- to reintroduce a sense of the Christmas-Epiphany season by employing traditional symbols

Symbol

The primary symbols for this exercise are ritual actions and sacramentals: asking God's blessing on a space, sprinkling blessed water, and making the 19+C+M+B+97 symbol above the lintel of outside doors. If you're in a space that can't be marked, a piece of paper may be taped or pinned above the door and the symbol drawn on that.

Materials

- chalk
- paper (if it's not possible to write directly above a door)
- holy water in a bowl
- small sprig of greenery to sprinkle the holy water
- a candle to serve as the "Christ candle"
- a candle for each participant

Introduction

Prior to the twentieth century, Christmas did not last one day. The Twelve Days of Christmas (which now linger only in popular song) were celebrated between Christmas and Epiphany. They were called "Smoke Nights" because people went through their houses and barns burning incense to bless their homes in preparation for the new year. The word "epiphany" means "manifestation"; the feast celebrates how God revealed his Son to the world. After each room of the house was incensed and blessed, the father of the family took a piece of blessed chalk and wrote over the door of every room that led out from the house to the open:

19+C+M+B+97

This stood for "Anno Domini 1997— Caspar, Melchior, Balthasar" and meant that the three kings or magi in this year of our Lord 1997 (or whatever year) protected the house from all evil.

The rite in this session is adapted for use by ministry groups who meet on a regular basis—those who find community and a sense of family within the walls of a parish or catechetical center. It explores the Catholic belief that "sacred space" can be created virtually anywhere, for Christ is present where two or more are gathered in his name. Drawing strength from each other, the members of Christ's family can go out to manifest his light to the world.

Exercises

Read and discuss the following quotations:

1. From the general introduction to *The Book of Blessings*:

As the Church, through the working of the Holy Spirit, fulfills its many-sided ministry of sanctifying, it has accordingly established many forms of blessing. Through them it calls us to praise God, encourages us to implore his protection, exhorts us to seek his mercy by our holiness of life, and provides us with ways of praying that God will grant the favors we ask. The blessings instituted by the Church are included among those signs perceptible to the senses by which human sanctification in Christ and the glorification of God are "signified and brought about in ways proper to each of these signs."...The Church in celebrating its blessings praises the Lord and implores divine grace at important moments in the life of its members. At times the Church also invokes blessings on objects and places connected with human occupations or activities and those related to the liturgy or to piety and popular devotions. But such blessings are invoked always with a view to the people who use the objects to be blessed and frequent the places to be blessed. God has given into our use and care the good things he has created, and we are also the recipients of his own wisdom. Thus the celebration of blessings becomes the means for us to profess that as we make use of what God has created we wish to find him and to love and serve him with all fidelity (xxv-xxvi)

2. From the foreword to *Catholic Household Blessings & Prayers*:

This book is devoted to that "bond of prayer" that joins the prayer of the Sunday assembly to the daily prayers of every Catholic....Along with other signs— the cross, holy water, blessed candles—

the presence of the Bible and this book of prayers expresses a way of life. This Catholic way—a way of daily justice, or service, and of care that is found around the family table and around the world's wide table—is our baptismal charge. It is the garment we put on at Baptism; we are clothed with Christ (3).

- Why do we bless ordinary objects and spaces?

- How can work places and gathering places become "sacred space" by symbols and ritual gestures?
- Why are these symbols and gestures such an important part of our Catholic heritage?
- Why do people instinctively think in terms of rituals and vows at the beginning of a new year?

Rite: Epiphany

The prayers in this rite are adapted from "Order for the Blessing of a Parish Hall or Catechetical Center" (*Book of Blessings*) and "Blessing of the Home and Household on the Epiphany" (*Catholic Household Blessings and Prayers*).

LEADER:
In the name of the Father, and of the Son, and of the Holy Spirit.

ALL:
Amen.

LEADER:
Peace be within these walls and with all who gather here.

ALL:
Amen.

LEADER:
During these days of the Christmas season, we keep this feast of Epiphany, celebrating the manifestation of Christ to the Magi, to John in the River Jordan, and to the disciples at the wedding at Cana. Today Christ is manifest to us! Today this is a holy place.

READER 1:
(*Read Eph 2:19-22.*)

READER 2:
(*Read Ps 72:1-2,7-8,10-11,12-13.*)

ALL:
Lord, every nation on earth will adore you.

READER 3:
(*Read Mt 2:1-2.*)

LEADER:
(*Preparing to bless the chalk*) Our help is in the name of the Lord.

ALL:
Now and forever.

LEADER:
Lord God, bless this chalk, mined from the earth you created. Render it holy as we inscribe the names of the saints Caspar, Melchior, and Balthasar upon the lintel of the door. Make it a symbol of the faith of the three kings, who allowed neither physical hardship nor the tyranny of Herod to deter them from seeking the Christ child. May those who enter this door find peace and fellowship within. May those who leave by this door journey courageously through the world to serve you.

(**LEADER** *inscribes the symbol 19+C+M+B+97 above the door leading to the outside of the building. Then* **ALL** *move throughout the meeting space. God's blessing is asked on all that takes place in that space. Holy water is sprinkled using a sprig of fresh greenery.*)

LEADER:
With praise and thanksgiving, let us ask God, through whom all things are accomplished, to bless this place.

ALL:
Hear us, O Lord.

LEADER:
For the Church, that all who are baptized may renew their commitment to Christ, we pray to the Lord.

ALL:
Hear us, O Lord.

LEADER:
For our ministry, that God may continue to

bless all our works in this new year, we pray to the Lord.

ALL:
Hear us, O Lord.

LEADER:
For those who gather within this space, that they may deepen their commitment to you and to each other as the people of God, we pray to the Lord.

ALL:
Hear us, O Lord.

LEADER:
Through our gathering together as "family" may we clearly discern our own gifts and ministries. May those gifts witness Christ's light to the world.

ALL:
Hear us, O Lord.

LEADER:
Just as Christ became a light to the gentiles when the magi came to do him homage, so may our lives witness Christ's light to all we meet.

ALL:
Hear us, O Lord.

LEADER:
(Light the Christ candle. Spontaneous intercessions may be spoken at this point.)

LEADER:
Jesus gathers us together as a family and calls us to pray.

ALL:
Our Father...

LEADER:

> Lord, God of heaven and earth,
> you revealed your only begotten Son
>   to every nation
> by the guidance of a star.
> Bless this place
> and all who meet within its walls.
> Fill us with the light of Christ,
> that our concern for others
>   may reflect your love.
> We ask this through Christ our Lord.

ALL:
Amen.

(Participants go forward and light their candles from the Christ candle. Conclude with "We Three Kings" or other appropriate Epiphany song.)

5. THE HOLY NAME OF JESUS

Season or Occasion

- a retreat to "kick off" the New Year
- an exploration of the names and nature of Jesus for teens and those engaged in the catechumenate during any season

Purpose

- to encourage a closer relationship with Jesus by choosing one aspect of his nature that attracts participants on a personal level

Symbol

The symbol is the traditional sign for the holy name of Jesus. Participants hang their favorite names of Jesus around it.

Materials

- image of the holy name of Jesus
- backdrop of gold lame fabric
- a blank 4" x 5" posterboard nametag for each participant with a piece of ribbon tied at the top large enough to hang around the neck
- crayons or colored pencils
- large bowl

Introduction

Although the Feast of the Holy Name of Jesus is no longer celebrated on the first Sunday following January 1, this exercise is an inspirational way to start the new year.

Traditional devotion to the holy name of Jesus was popularized by the Franciscan preacher, St. Bernardino of Siena (1380-1444). After preaching repentance, Bernardino kindled popular fervor by displaying a tablet painted with the initials I.H.S. (the first three letters of the Greek translation of "Jesus") surrounded by rays. He blessed the crowds (up to thirty thousand) with this image of the holy name of Jesus. It was emblazoned on his missionary banner. Morals were reformed, sinners converted and "bonfires of the vanities" consumed penitents' luxury items.

However, Bernardino ran into a snag in Bologna when he persuaded this "Las Vegas of Italy" to burn its cards and dice in the public square. "You've ruined my only source of income!" wailed a local card manufacturer. The quick-witted Bernardino told the man to take tablets inscribed with the holy name of Jesus. The excited crowd bought more sacred monograms than they had ever bought playing cards.

St. Bernardino also wrote of his devotion to the name of Jesus in "On the Song of Songs:"

The name of Jesus is not only light, but it is also food....The name of Jesus is honey in the mouth, music to the ear, a cry of gladness in the heart!...Do we feel sad? Let the name of Jesus come into our heart.... Do we fall into sin? Does despair even urge us to suicide? Let us but invoke this life-giving name and our will to live be at once renewed. The hardness of heart... apathy bred of indolence, bitterness of mind, repugnance for the things of the spirit— have they ever failed to yield in the presence of that saving name?...And where is the one who, tossed on the rolling waves of doubt, did not quickly find certitude by recourse to...Jesus' name? Was ever a person so discouraged, so beaten down by affliction, to whom the sound of this name did not bring new resolve? In short, for all the ills and disorders to which flesh is heir this name is medicine. For proof we have no less than his own promise, "Call upon me in the day of trouble, I will deliver you, and you shall glorify me."...For when I name Jesus... this same man is the all-powerful God whose way of life heals me, whose support is my strength (quoted by Pennington and Katzir)

Exercises

1. Hand out the following list of the names of Jesus to each participant.

   Advocate (1 Jn 2:1)
   Alpha & Omega (Rev 22:13)
   Author of Life (Acts 3:15)
   Bread of Life (Jn 6:35)
   Captain of Salvation (Heb 2:10)
   Cornerstone (Eph 2:19-21)
   Daystar (2 Pet 1:19)

   Deliverer (Rom 11:26)
   Emmanuel (Mt 1:23)
   Eternal Life (1 Jn 5:20)
   Firstborn of the Dead (Col 1:18)
   Good Shepherd (Jn 10:11-14)
   Great High Priest (Heb 4:14)
   Head of the Church (Eph 5:23)
   King of Kings & Lord of Lords
      (1 Tim 6:14-16)

Lamb of God (Jn 1:29)

Light of the World (Jn 8:12)

Lord (Phil 2:10-11)

Master (Jn 13:13)

Messiah (Jn 1:41)

Our Passover (1 Cor 5:7)

Resurrection and Life (Jn 11:25-26)

Rising Sun (Lk 1:77-79)

Savior (Lk 2:11)

Son of God (Mt 26:63-64)

True Vine (Jn 15:1)

Way, Truth, Life (Jn 14:6)

Word of Life (1 Jn 1:1)

2. Each person chooses his or her favorite name of Jesus and looks up the appropriate Scripture reference in the Bible.

3. Each takes a blank nametag, draws the chosen name of Jesus plus a symbol representing that name on the front, and signs his or her name on the back.

4. Discuss why each name of Jesus was chosen.

- What does it mean in Scripture? In our lives?
- How can we embrace that aspect of Jesus this year and call on it to give us strength?

Rite: The Holy Name of Jesus

LEADER:

In the Name of the Father, and of the Son, and of the Holy Spirit.

ALL:

Amen.

LEADER:

The name of the LORD
    is a strong tower;
the righteous run into it
    and are safe (Prv 18:10).

There is salvation in no one else, for there is no other name under heaven given among mortals by which we must be saved (Acts 4:12).

Therefore God also highly exalted him
    and gave him the name
    that is above every name,
so that at the name of Jesus
    every knee should bend,...
and every tongue should confess
    that Jesus Christ is Lord,
    to the glory of God the Father
    (Phil 2:9-11).

Amen.

(While the "Litany of the Holy Name" [abbreviated, from A Book of Prayers] is read, each participant approaches the bowl placed under the image of the name of Jesus, bows his or her head reverently, places a name tag in the bowl, and returns to his or her seat. The Litany may be read by the LEADER, by several readers, alternative lines read by Group 1 and Group 2, etc.)

ALL:

Lord, have mercy

Christ, have mercy

Lord, have mercy

God our Father in heaven,
    have mercy on us
God the Son, Redeemer of the world,
    have mercy on us
God the Holy Spirit, have mercy on us
Holy Trinity, one God, have mercy on us

Jesus, Son of the living God,
    have mercy on us
Jesus, splendor of the Father,
    have mercy on us
Jesus, brightness of everlasting light
    have mercy on us
Jesus, king of glory, have mercy on us
Jesus, dawn of justice, have mercy on us
Jesus, Son of the Virgin Mary,
    have mercy on us
Jesus, mighty God, have mercy on us
Jesus all-powerful, have mercy on us
Jesus pattern of patience,
    have mercy on us
Jesus, model of obedience,
    have mercy on us

Jesus, lover of us all, have mercy on us
Jesus, God of peace, have mercy on us
Jesus, author of life, have mercy on us
Jesus, our God, have mercy on us
Jesus, our refuge, have mercy on us
Jesus, father of the poor,
    have mercy on us
Jesus, treasure of the faithful,
    have mercy on us

Jesus, Good Shepherd, have mercy on us
Jesus, the true light, have mercy on us
Jesus, eternal wisdom, have mercy on us

Jesus, infinite goodness, have mercy on us
Jesus, our way and our life,
   have mercy on us
Jesus, king of patriarchs,
   have mercy on us
Jesus, teacher of apostles,
   have mercy on us
Jesus, master of evangelists,
   have mercy on us
Jesus, courage of martyrs,
   have mercy on us
Jesus, crown of all saints,
   have mercy on us

From all evil, Jesus, save your people
From every sin, Jesus, save your people
From everlasting death,
   Jesus, save your people

By the mystery of your incarnation,
   Jesus, save your people
By your hidden life,
   Jesus, save your people
By your agony and crucifixion,
   Jesus, save your people
By your rising to new life,
   Jesus, save your people
By your return in glory to the Father,
   Jesus, save your people

Lamb of God, you take away the sins
   of the world,
   have mercy on us
Lamb of God, you take away the sins
   of the world,
   have mercy on us
Lamb of God, you take away the sins
   of the world,
   have mercy on us

Amen.

LEADER:
(Take each tag from the bowl and read: "N. chooses the Good Shepherd," "N. chooses the Bread of Life," etc. Each person has his or her name tag hung around his or her neck and stands in a circle around the Name of Jesus symbol.)

ALL:
During this coming year, I place myself under the care of Jesus Christ.

   Our help is in the name of the LORD
    who made heaven and earth
    (Ps 124:8).

(Sing the hymn, "At the Name of Jesus.")

6. THE CHURCH OF THE LOCKED DOOR

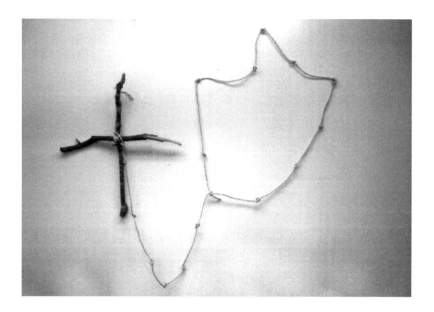

Season or Occasion

- The Church of the Locked Door: The Underground Church in Times of Persecution
- Lent

Purpose

- to help us not take freedom of worship for granted

Symbol

The symbol for this exercise is an abbreviated "prison rosary" made from coarse rope and a cross made from two pieces of stick lashed together. One large "prison rosary" hangs on the wall; each participant makes his or her own miniature "prison rosary." It is the cross at its most elemental level. Rope helps us recall the ordinary materials Jesus worked with as a carpenter and the material he was bound with when flogged during his Passion.

This cross is stripped of all frills; so must our spiritual lives be simplified. This cross is fashioned with ingenuity from existing materials; so must we witness with ingenuity as church. We can't wait for ideal conditions and fancy teaching aids, but we must work with what we have.

Materials

- wall "prison rosary": coarse rope and a cross made of two sticks lashed together
- a large piece of paper and felt-tip pen for the "iron bars" image used in this session's rite
- individual "prison rosaries" made of rough twine and tiny crosses made of twigs and twine for each participant (Note: Supply enough materials to make two rosaries per person, one to make during the first exercise and the second to be distributed during the rite)
- a Bible for each participant

Introduction

A perfect example of The Church of the Locked Door—faith at its most basic—is the story of two American hostages held by Beirut terrorists: Terry Anderson and Fr. Martin Jenco, OSM. Fr. Jenco was imprisoned for nineteen months (January 1985 to July 1986) while Terry Anderson was held captive for six years and nine months (March 16, 1985, to December 4, 1991). Both men were chained to a wall in the same room for an entire year.

A lapsed Catholic, Anderson had decided to return to the church a few months before his abduction. After being snatched by terrorists, it was his faith that sustained him through the ordeal.

Fr. Jenco recalled: "I was chained in a clothes closet with a plastic bag on my head. But I could look through a crack and see a man chained to a bed, traumatized and weeping. Sometimes they would mock him."

Anderson prayed, read the Bible, and drew strength from his fellow prisoners in what they called "The Church of the Locked Door." Anderson made rosaries from strings pulled from a mat and Muslim prayer-beads; Fr. Jenco made his from potato sack strings. "It was the one thing they never took away from me," Anderson recalled. "I was deathly afraid I'd lose it, because every time we moved I lost something. Whenever I felt like, geez, something's going to happen, I'd quickly grab the rosary and wrap it around my wrist and I'd wear it for days, weeks....I remember a guard one day trying to take it off me and I said no." Pushing the rosary farther up his arm, Anderson allowed the guard to tape his wrists for another ride in the car trunk to a new prison. He carried that rosary back to freedom when he was released.

Fr. Jenco was a Servite, a member of the Order of Friar Servants of Mary, which promotes the Rosary of the Sorrowful Mother. During his imprisonment, Fr. Jenco sometimes counted his prayers on the links of his chains. "I made my own mysteries up, too. I would tie into different persons in Scripture." To the sorrowful mysteries he added the sorrows of abandonment by his friends. "After being a hostage, I touch my rosary differently now....Rosaries are a way of tying into God's creation because you touch metal or wood or stone. Touching is part of prayer that we sometimes forget. Touch a bead and just feel it" (quoted by Feister).

Exercises

1. Picture yourself imprisoned for your faith in Nazi Germany, Communist Russia, Ancient Rome, or any other time or place. Make a rough "prison rosary" from coarse twine or rope and two sticks lashed together. Describe the thoughts and feelings this symbol invokes.

2. Picture yourself imprisoned for your faith. Other prisoners who have never heard of Jesus turn to you for hope and inspiration. The guards are coming to take you away to an unknown fate. You may never see these people again. In five minutes, present the essence of your faith to your fellow prisoners.

3. Picture yourself imprisoned for your faith. All Christian books and symbols are forbidden. However, a fellow prisoner manages to slip you a Bible. Suddenly, you hear that you've been betrayed: the guards are coming to seize all contraband religious materials. Under a deadline of five min-

utes, choose the Bible passage that is most meaningful to you. Read this passage to the group and explain why you chose it to sustain you in your imprisonment.

4. If any participants have witnessed to their faith against great odds, they may wish to share their stories with the group.

Rite: The Church of the Locked Door

LEADER:

In the Name of the Father, and of the Son, and of the Holy Spirit.

ALL:

Amen.

LEADER:

We gather here as companions in Christ. Each day we try to bring the message of Christ to a world that is indifferent or openly hostile.

> We are warriors now, fighting on the battlefield of faith, and God sees all we do; the angels watch and so does Christ.

ALL:

> What honor and glory and joy, to do battle in the presence of God.

LEADER:

> Let us arm ourselves in full strength and prepare ourselves for the ultimate struggle with blameless hearts, true faith, and undying courage.

ALL:

> What honor and glory and joy, to do battle in the presence of God ("Common of Several Martyrs," *Liturgy of the Hours*).

READER 1:

(Read 1 Pet 4:13-14.)

READER 2:

(Read Mt 5:1-2.)

ALL:

(Read the Beatitude Mt 5:11 either in unison, alternating Group A and Group B, or in whatever creative fashion LEADER desires.)

READER 3:

(Read 2 Cor 4:7-11.)

(LEADER directs the group's attention to the large piece of paper displaying the iron bars image:)

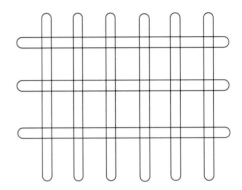

LEADER:

These iron bars are a symbol of the forces that imprison our world. At times these bars appear to be impossible to break. However, Jesus has told us how these bars can be dissolved. *(Draw a heart around the iron bars and place a cross at the top.)*

LEADER:

(Read Jn 15:9-17.)

The way to dissolve these iron bars is to follow the cross in love. And when you see that these bars are actually the cross

(blacken the center bars, revealing these bars to be tiny crosses), the bars dissolve and disappear.

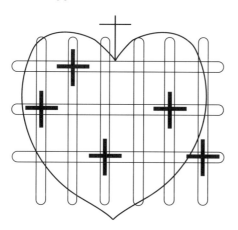

St. Paul tells us in 1 Corinthians 4:10-13,

We are fools for the sake of Christ, but you are wise in Christ. We are weak, but you are strong. You are held in honor, but we in disrepute. To the present hour we are hungry and thirsty, we are poorly clothed and beaten and homeless, and we grow weary from the work of our own hands. When reviled, we bless; when persecuted, we endure; when slandered, we speak kindly.

As one Body in Christ, let us join hands. United in love, we can break any prison fetters by saying: "We are fools for the sake of Christ."

ALL:
(Stand in a circle, hands joined) We are fools for the sake of Christ.

LEADER:
By preaching the Gospel in the face of political oppression...

ALL:
We are fools for the sake of Christ.

LEADER:
By standing together against violence...

ALL:
We are fools for the sake of Christ.

LEADER: By working to eliminate child abuse...

ALL:
We are fools for the sake of Christ.

LEADER:
(Add as many "iron bars" as seem appropriate. LEADER may also request spontaneous "iron bars" from the participants. When the prayers are complete, ALL recite the "Our Father." Then LEADER indicates the "prison rosary" symbol hanging on the wall. Under it is a bowl of tiny "prison rosaries" to be given to participants. LEADER explains that, as a sign of our commitment to preaching the Good News to the troubled world, each person will walk forward to receive a miniature "prison rosary" and a scroll. While appropriate music is played, each person walks forward. LEADER says, "We are fools for the sake of Christ" and the participant responds, "Amen." The participant receives a tiny "prison rosary" and a scroll on which is printed one of the Scripture quotations used in this rite. The scroll is tied with rough twine. When ALL have returned to their seats, LEADER says:) Each of you now has two "prison rosaries"—the one you made and the one you received during this prayer service. We charge you to give one of these rosaries to someone else as your witness to bring the Good News. May God who has begun the good works in you bring it to completion.

ALL:
Amen.

(In conclusion, sing "A Mighty Fortress is Our God" or some other suitably inspiring tune.)

7. TRUE VINE

Season or Occasion

- Ordinary Time
- Holy Name of Jesus
- True Vine

Purpose

- to allow participants to integrate the aspect of Christ and the church as True Vine into their lives and ministries

Symbol

The pilgrim cross is the core symbol for several sessions in this book. If you lead a group that meets over a period of time, introduce this symbol at the very first meeting as a personal "mascot" for each participant. As the liturgical calendar unwinds, the cross remains as the central symbol: its trappings change to match each season.

Materials

- cross made of wood
- materials to fasten cross pieces together
- a long strand of artificial ivy

Introduction

"For there is hope for a tree,
   if it is cut down, that it will sprout
    again,
  and that its shoots will not cease.
Though its root grows old in the earth,
   and its stump dies in the ground,
yet at the scent of water it will bud
   and put forth branches like a young
    plant (Job 14:7-9).

Every Catholic experiences times of drought, desert experiences, periods of dryness in prayer. Yet hope helps us grit our teeth and endure those times when—like Job's tree—our roots grow old and die. By clinging to faith and its symbols, we endure until the scent of water makes our faith bud and blossom again. These times of rebirth teach us the lesson that Albert Camus wrote of: "In the midst of winter, I discover in myself an invincible summer."

Exercises

1. Each participant creates his or her own pilgrim cross either from two small tree limbs lashed together with rope or wire or from boards nailed together. It should be small enough to be easily handled but large enough to decorate and "interact with." Interestingly, large symbols take on an almost human presence when worked with over time and therefore become more and more effective. When the cross is assembled, have each person wind a long strand of artificial greenery or ivy around it (purchased from a local craft store).

2. Read and discuss John 15:5-8.

   • What does Christ's role as True Vine mean to each participant on a personal level?

3. Read 1 Corinthians 12:1-26.

   • How does the concept of "True Vine" model the church?
   • How can we, as individuals, become fruitful vines?
   • What are the withered, stunted branches that must be pruned from our lives?
   • What role do the sacraments, our ministry, our prayer life, our community life, play in this pruning?
   • Is the soil we live in rich or barren? How can we nourish this soil? How can we become, in turn, nourishing soil in which other "vines" may flourish?

Rite: True Vine

(In the center of the space stands a large cross made of tree limbs or wooden planks. The cross is bare, but at its foot sits a bowl filled with pieces of artificial vine, just like the vines that the participants twined around their own individual crosses. Another bowl holds packets of seeds. As the rite begins, ALL gather around the bare cross.)

LEADER:
In the name of the Father, and of the Son, and of the Holy Spirit.

READER 1:
(Read Jn 15:1-17.)

READER 2:
A reading from St. Cyril of Jerusalem:

> Let us therefore bear fruit
> as we should!
> Let our fate be not that of the barren
> fig tree;
> let Jesus not come again today
> to curse it for its barrenness!
>
> May we all say: "As for me,
> like a green olive tree in the house
> of God,
> I have forever put my hope in the
> mercy of God!"
> An olive tree that is not material
> but spiritual, a bearer of light.
>
> It is for God, then, to plant and water
> but for you to bear fruit;
> for God to give his grace
> but for you to receive and preserve it.

READER 3:
A reading from St. Catherine of Siena:

> You then are my workers; you
> have come from me, the supreme
> eternal gardener, and I have grafted

you onto the vine by making myself one with you. Keep in mind that each of you has your own vineyard. But everyone is joined to your neighbors' vineyards without any dividing lines. They are so joined together, in fact, that you cannot do good or evil for yourself without doing the same for your neighbors. All of you together make up one common vineyard, the whole Christian assembly, and you are all united in the vineyard of the mystic body of holy church from which you draw your life (Noffke 62).

READER 4:
A reading from Theodore of Studios:

> How splendid the cross of Christ!
> It brings life, not death;
> light, not darkness;
> Paradise, not its loss.
> It is the wood on which the Lord,
> like a great warrior,
> was wounded in hands and feet
> and side,
> but healed thereby our wounds.
> A tree had destroyed us,
> a tree now brought us life.

LEADER:
We are all united in Christ as part of the True Vine.

(Each participant walks forward, takes a piece of vine from the bowl, and wraps it around the bare cross. Each person is then given a packet of seed before returning to his or her seat.)

(As the above proceeds, ALL sing a song on the theme of new life, unity, and ministry.)

8. ST. PATRICK

Good Shepherd image courtesy of Jamie Aven, San Antonio, Texas. Shepherd's crook courtesy of Keith Foegelle, Corpus Christi, Texas.

Season or Occasion

- Feast of St. Patrick, Patron of Youth, March 17
- any youth gathering

Purpose

- to provide a strong, courageous role model for teens

Symbol

The symbol for St. Patrick begins with the image of the Good Shepherd with shepherd's staff and cloak (see session 9). To that symbol add a shamrock and St. Patrick's Breastplate bracelets.

Materials

- green felt or construction paper for shamrock
- green craft beads
- inexpensive St. Patrick medals (see your local church store to buy in bulk)
- rawhide thong/craft cord

Introduction

St. Patrick had it all: money, a father in local politics, slaves, and good times. Patrick had everything—except interest in the church. Until the barbarians kidnapped him from his home in Britain and sold him into slavery in Ireland. The son of a slave owner had become a slave himself.

The youth who had never worked a day in his life found himself trudging the cold mountain pastures of his pagan master, tending sheep. Patrick had lost everything. But he found God. Friendless and more alone than he had ever been before, Patrick began to pray: every day, many times a day.

After six years of slavery, Patrick dreamed that God told him a ship was ready to take him home. Escaping his captors, Patrick trudged two hundred miles to the coast—living on scraps, sleeping on the ground, dodging pursuit.

Yet when he reached the coast, his plea for passage was rejected by the ship's captain. Patrick desperately prayed for help. "Come quickly!" shouted a crew member. Patrick escaped from Ireland on a ship filled with Irish wolfhounds to be sold as hunters of wild game. Patrick the Hunted had become Patrick the Free.

Yet Patrick was not free of God's call to ministry. Safely home, he dreamed of the voices of the Irish who had enslaved him. "Come walk with us!" they cried. Patrick woke, and knew he was no longer the selfish, spoiled, rich man's son. He would become a priest and return to Ireland in God's name. "I was very moved in my heart," he wrote in his *Confessions* as an old man, an archbishop. "Thank God that after many years the Lord answered my cry."

Exercises

1. Assemble Good Shepherd image, staff, and cloak (see next session). Cut shamrocks from green felt or construction paper. Create St. Patrick's Breastplate bracelets by stringing three green beads (three for the Trinity, shamrock green for Ireland) and a St. Patrick medal on craft cord, knotting before and after each item to keep in place.

2. St. Patrick (c. 389-461) was about sixteen when he was kidnapped by raiders and sold as a slave. He knew abuse, hunger, fear, loneliness. He had been on the run—an alien, a homeless transient. Yet he heard God's voice and returned safely to his family around the age of twenty-two.

   - Do any of these facts about Patrick appeal to you?
   - Can you find parallels in your own life?

   - Do you think St. Patrick would understand your problems if you brought them to him?

3. Although Patrick was abused, he didn't abuse others. Instead, thanks to prayer and trust in God, he returned to the place that enslaved him and helped others.

   - Does his example have any meaning in your own life?
   - What steps can you take to heal past hurts in your life?
   - Can you learn from these healed hurts and help others with that knowledge?

4. St. Patrick didn't minister to the Irish alone. He tramped the wilderness with his friends: priests, bodyguards, cooks, artists, seminarians. Patrick's friends could build a church from the ground up every

time they stopped to rest, just as Roman soldiers could create a camp. Legends say that Patrick's charioteer even took a blow from a pagan lance intended for his bishop. These friends supported Patrick's battle against pagan gangs that massacred new converts to Christianity. Outraged at one rogue pagan leader called Coroticus, Patrick wrote of the "newly baptized, anointed with chrism, in white garments, they had been slain. Did I come to Ireland without God? Is it of my own doing that I have holy mercy on the people who once took me captive? I was free-born, but I sold my noble rank for the good of others. Thus, I am a slave to Christ in a foreign nation. I grieve for you, dearly beloved."

• Have you ever grieved for those injured by gang violence?
• Can you unite with your friends and ask God's support in fighting violence and abuse today?

Rite: St. Patrick

(Readings are taken from the "Mass for the Feast of St. Patrick," March 17).

(The wonderful words of the prayer of St. Patrick used in this session have been set to music as a hymn of the Episcopal church. "St. Patrick's Breastplate" or "Hymn 370" (theme: the Holy Trinity) is available in The Hymnal (New York: The Church Hymnal Corporation, 1982 and The Church Pension Fund, 1985); it can also be found in any traditional Episcopal hymnal and is in the index under the first line: "I bind unto myself today." If your music ministers can sing this or tape and play it during the rite of receiving the bracelets, it will add great beauty to the symbolism.)

LEADER:
In the name of the Father, and of the Son, and of the Holy Spirit.

ALL:
Amen.

READER 1:
(Read 1 Pet 4:7-11.)

READER 2:
(Read Ps 96:1-2,2-3,7-8,10.)

ALL:
R. Proclaim his marvelous deeds to all the nations.

READER 3:
(Read Lk 5:1-11.)

LEADER:
A famous prayer is attributed to St. Patrick, called "St. Patrick's Breastplate." A breastplate is a piece of armor that protected a warrior. St. Patrick recited his prayer for protection while marching though forests filled with violent pagan gangs. This prayer will be recited while each of you walks forward to receive a St. Patrick's Breastplate bracelet. *(Hold up bracelet.)* The three green beads of the bracelet remind us of the Trinity, which St. Patrick thought was symbolized by the Irish shamrock. The St. Patrick medal reminds us that he received God's help and protection during times of pain and fear.

ALL:
(Walk forward and receive the bracelet on wrists. Next recite the prayer. If participants are too young to handle the traditional language of the prayer, LEADER may recite it.)

I bind unto myself today
the strong name of the Trinity:
By invocation of the same,
The Three in One and One in Three.

I bind unto myself this day
by power of faith,
    Christ's incarnation,
His baptism in the Jordan River,
His death on the Cross
    for my salvation.
His bursting from the spiced tomb,
His riding up the heavenly way,
His coming at the day of doom.

I bind unto myself this day
The power of God to hold and lead:
His eye to watch, His might to stay,
His ear to harken to my need;
The wisdom of my God to teach,
His hand to guide,
    His shield to ward;
The Word of God
    to give me speech,
His heavenly host to be my guard!

Christ be with me, Christ within me,
Christ behind me, Christ before me,
Christ beside me, Christ to win me,
Christ to comfort and restore me.
Christ beneath me,
    Christ above me,
Christ in quiet, Christ in danger,
Christ in hearts of all that love me,
Christ in mouth of friend
    and stranger.

I bind unto myself the name,
The strong name of the Trinity:
By invocation of the same,
The Three in One and One in Three;
of whom all nature has creation,
Eternal Father, Spirit, Word;
Praise to the Lord of my salvation —
Salvation is of Christ the Lord!

LEADER:
(*After* ALL *have received bracelets, lead the participants in miming the gestures of the "Christ text" that begins: "Christ be with me, Christ within me...Christ in mouth of friend and stranger." Continue with:*)

Let us pray.

St. Patrick changed from shepherd to good shepherd, caring for the flock that enslaved him. Let us also forgive those who harm us. Sin and violence infested Ireland like snakes, but Patrick drove them out. Let us cast out the serpents of sin in our own lives. And like St. Patrick the missionary, let us fearlessly witness God's love to the world.

ALL:
Amen.

9. THE GOOD SHEPHERD

Good Shepherd image courtesy of Jamie Aven, San Antonio, Texas.
Shepherd's crook courtesy of Keith Foegelle, Corpus Christi, Texas.

Season or Occasion

- Good Shepherd Sunday
- any occasion when participants need to feel cherished and protected by Jesus

Purpose

- to explore the loving, protective aspect of Christ through his name "the Good Shepherd"

Materials

Arrange on the table in the middle of the group:

- a shepherd's cloak made of rough brown fabric

- an image of the Good Shepherd (if you can't manage a Good Shepherd, use a lamb)
- a shepherd's crook or crosier. (One can be quickly traced on cardboard and cut out. However, since this symbol can be used for many different exercises, one cut from a wooden board, sanded, and stained is ideal.)

Preparation

Have ready in a bowl a mini-symbol for each participant. This consists of a small square of the rough fabric used for the shepherd's cloak and a shepherd's crook made from a brown pipe cleaner. (Attach both with a few stitches or a safety pin.)

46

Introduction

This session has many possible uses. Catechumenate leaders can use it for Good Shepherd Sunday or as a christology exercise to help catechumens in their ongoing relationship with Jesus. It is also suitable year-round as a liturgy for those undergoing pain, sorrow, or transition. The prayer in this session's rite reassures participants that God cares for us as a shepherd cared for his sheep in the ancient world.

The Good Shepherd is everywhere in the early Christian catacombs. The early Christians preferred the image of a beardless youth in a short tunic bearing a lamb on his shoulders: a figure of no political power but infinitely caring. A shepherd knew each of his sheep by name and they answered to special calls. He protected them with his life, living in the wilderness, fighting off wolves with his shepherd's crook (now the crosier carried by our bishops as a symbol of their pastoral role. The Latin word *pastor* means "shepherd" or, literally, "he who feeds the sheep and takes them to pasture"). Shepherds often built corrals of earth topped with thorns and slept across the open doorway to fend off wolves. Thus the shepherd *was* the door, explaining Christ's meaning in John 10:1-16 when he calls himself first the door and then the shepherd.

Exercises

1. Ask participants what they think the symbol means or what it reminds them of.

2. Have all participants read John 10:1-16.

3. Discuss how Jesus has been a caring Shepherd in each person's life. If the person feels that the Shepherd has been lacking in his or her life, ask him or her to describe how he or she pictures the Shepherd's comfort and loving care.

4. Ask each person to write down a special intention he or she wishes to place in the care of the Good Shepherd. Have each roll the paper into a scroll, tie it with ribbon, and write his or her name on it. (If you choose this session for the benefit of one person or family who is going through tough times, there is an alternate way of doing the rite. Let participants create prayer scrolls praying for the needs of that one person and/or family instead of their own. These can be pinned to the cloak and given to the person in need. Those with embroidery skills could also embroider each Scripture reference (e.g., Jn 21:17) on the cloak, providing a blanket of protection.) After the rite, give the cloak to the person in need as a token of the Good Shepherd's care and love. It can be hung on the wall or placed over a sick bed.

Rite: The Good Shepherd

(ALL *gather in a circle around the table holding the Good Shepherd symbol. Light a candle on the table.*)

LEADER:
In the name of the Father, and of the Son, and of the Holy Spirit.

ALL:
Amen.

LEADER:
The Lord is my shepherd, I shall not want.

ALL:
(*Read Ps 23.*)

(*For the following, you may use one reader or various readers.*)

READER:
(*Read Ezek 34:11,12,14,16.*)

ALL:
The Lord is my shepherd, I shall not want.

READER:
(*Read Jn 10:14-16.*)

ALL:
The Lord is my shepherd, I shall not want.

READER:
(*Read Jn 21:17.*)

ALL:
The Lord is my shepherd, I shall not want.

READER:
(*Read Isa 53:6,7,11*).

ALL:
The Lord is my shepherd, I shall not want.

LEADER:
We are the flock of the Good Shepherd, the Lamb of God who takes away the sins of the world. Let us place our fears and needs under his loving care. (*Explain how*

each person is to walk forward, place the scroll on the cloak of the Good Shepherd, and receive the mini Good Shepherd symbol in return as ALL *recite the following prayer. After the* LEADER *reads each line of the prayer,* ALL *repeat the words, "The Lord is my shepherd, I shall not want."*)

He is the Paschal of our salvation.
It is he who endured many
    things:
It is he that was in Abel murdered.
And in Isaac bound, and in Jacob
    exiled,
and in Joseph sold, and in Moses
    exposed,
and in the lamb slain, and in David
    persecuted,
and in the prophets dishonored.
It is he that was enfleshed
    in a virgin,
that was hanged on a tree,
that was buried in the earth,
that was raised from the dead,
that was taken up to the heights of
the heavens.
He is the lamb being slain;
he is the lamb that was speechless;
he is the one born from Mary
    the lovely ewe-lamb;
he is the one taken from the flock,
and dragged to slaughter,
    and sacrificed at evening,
and buried at night;
who on the tree was not broken,
in the earth was not dissolved,
who arose from the dead,
and raised up mankind
    from the grave below
(Melito of Sardis, second century).

ALL:

(*Sing or recite:*)

Lamb of God, you take away
  the sins of the world;
  have mercy on us.
Lamb of God, you take away
  the sins of the world;
  have mercy on us.
Lamb of God, you take away
  the sins of the world;
  grant us peace
(prepared by the International
Consultation on English Texts).

LEADER:

(*Read Rev 21:22-25.*)

ALL:

(*Sing "Crown Him with Many Crowns."*)

10. SIN BRICKS

Season or Occasion

- Lent
- catechumenate illustration of the sacrament of penance
- any occasion of repentance and reconciliation

Purpose

- to illustrate how sin creates barriers which reconciliation dissolves

Symbol

This consists of a life-sized drawing of a stone gateway big enough to walk through. (Making the gateway out of little, individually hand-cut construction paper "stones" is more effective but more time-consuming. You may want participants to help make the gateway as part of the exercise.) You may label the archway bricks as the Ten Commandments. The gateway is blocked by "sin bricks" of construction paper on which participants write their sins.

Materials

- large sheet of paper (rolls of brown paper for wrapping packages work well)
- black felt-tip pens to draw gateway and bricks
- construction paper to make a "sin brick" for each participant
- pins or tape to attach "sin bricks" easily to the "gateway"
- container in which to burn "sin bricks"
- matches

Introduction

Most people have heard the story in Luke 18:18-26 in which Jesus tells a rich man that it is hard for the wealthy to enter the kingdom of God. In fact, it is easier for a camel to go through the eye of a needle.

However, I once read that the Needle was a real gateway. It had an upper door and a lower door. In times of insecurity, the upper door was closed and the only way travelers could pass through the opening at the bottom was to drop to their knees and crawl through. While scholars dispute this interpretation, the image stuck in my mind as a graphic illustration of how hard the road to heaven can be. Sin creates a brick barrier (how harmless each brick seems!) that blocks our way to sainthood over time. The only way to get through is to literally drop to our knees.

Exercises

1. Read and discuss Luke 18:18-26. First discuss how being "rich" impedes our way to heaven, then substitute the word "sinful" for "rich" and discuss how sin has the same effect.

   - Are being "rich" and being "sinful" sometimes connected in our consumer-oriented, materialistic society?

2. Give each participant enough construction paper to create a "sin brick." If you have a small group and a big gateway, each person can make several "sin bricks." Have each person write his or her most troublesome fault or sin on the brick (they may conceal it on the back if they want to maintain privacy).

3. After pointing out how the gateway is large enough to walk through and is free of obstacles, have each person walk up and attach his or her "sin brick" in such a way as to obstruct and fill up the gateway. Discuss how small sins committed "brick by brick" can create immovable obstacles.

   - Can the combined sins of a group fill up the gateway even faster than the sins of an individual?
   - How does obedience to the Ten Commandments ward off "sin brick" blockades?

Rite: Sin Bricks

LEADER:
In the name of the Father, and of the Son, and of the Holy Spirit.

ALL:
Amen.

LEADER:
Lord, you loved all sinners.
You ate at their tables
   and stayed at their homes.
You called them to give up everything
   and follow you.
Call us now to confess our sins
   and be at peace in your presence.
Amen.

READER 1:
(Read Heb 12:5-7,11-13.)

READER 2:
(Read Ps 32.)

ALL:
R. Happy are those whose sins are forgiven.

READER 3:
(Read Lk 13:22-30.)

LEADER:
In recognition of our own failings, let us confess our sins in the presence of God and one another.

ALL:
(Pray the Confiteor from the Roman Missal;)

   I confess to almighty God,
   and to you my brothers and sisters,
   that I have sinned through my own
   fault, in my thoughts
     and in my words,
   in what I have done,
   and in what I have failed to do.

   And I ask blessed Mary ever virgin,
   all the angels and saints,
   and you, my brothers and sisters,
   to pray for me to the Lord our God.

LEADER:
Christ asked that we be reconciled to each other before approaching God's altar. Let us now give one another the sign of peace.

ALL:
(Exchange sign of peace and sing "Lamb of God.")

LEADER:
(Direct each participant to walk forward, remove his or her "sin brick" from the gateway, and say clearly: "Happy are those whose sins are forgiven" and place the "brick" in the nearby brazier. While this is taking place, a song of reconciliation is sung or played, for example, "Amazing Grace," "I Heard the Voice of Jesus Say," "Let us Break Bread Together." When all "sin bricks" are in the container and the gateway is once again clear, LEADER sets them on fire.)

ALL:
(Pray the Lord's Prayer.)

LEADER:
May God, who has begun the good work in you, bring it to fulfillment. Our prayer service is ended; let us go forth to serve God and each other.

ALL:
Amen.

(If a priest is available, the sacrament of penance may be celebrated at this time.)

11. BROKEN HEART

Season or Occasion

- Lent
- reconciliation
- healing

Purpose

- to explore with catechumens or retreat participants the themes of sin, purification, reconciliation, and renewal

Symbol

The symbol for this session is a broken heart pieced back together by many helping hands.

Materials

- construction paper or poster board: red for the heart, flesh-colored for the hands, white for background
- glue
- scissors
- felt-tip pens

Introduction

"As we commit sins, we break away from God and break into small pieces," Grace Sosa, religious education coordinator for the Diocese of Corpus Christi, tells me. She holds up a red paper heart and tears off a tiny piece. "People hurrying off to a retreat may argue with a spouse or cut too sharply in front of another car. A little piece of themselves may have broken off because of the retreat itself."

She tears off more tiny little pieces of the heart. "During Lent we look at the brokenness of Christ and the healing power behind his death and resurrection. In this season I ask myself, 'Where have I broken? How can I heal that brokenness and continue to grow from it?'"

During this exercise, Grace cuts a red paper heart into small pieces to create a puzzle. Then she gives the puzzle to her retreat participants to solve as a group, having added extra pieces to make it even more challenging. "Each person is given a piece and must work together with the others to make one complete heart," she explains. "One person can't hog all the pieces in a corner by themselves. If they do, the broken heart will never be put back together again."

The retreat participants also make "healing hands" from construction paper and write on each hand the qualities that bring about healing of the wounds of sin: love, faith, trust, patience, repentance, reconciliation, etc.

The sacrament of penance is a vital part of this healing process. "It's easy to say 'I'm sorry' to a person and not mean it," says Grace. "But when the priest acts as Jesus in the sacrament, we're really talking to Jesus, face to face. That's why we don't want to go into that reconciliation room. Some of us are afraid, feeling the guilt and shame and afraid we can't be forgiven. But God forgives us. We need to go to that priest and make that confession because he is acting as Christ, and there is such a healing sense of power."

Exercises

1. Have participants create a "broken heart" by drawing a large red heart on poster board and cutting it into puzzle pieces. Add extra pieces to make putting the puzzle together more challenging. If you have a large group, you may wish to create several "broken hearts" and split the group into smaller clusters to interact.

2. Have participants create "healing hands" by tracing their own hands and cutting out the drawings. Have each person label his or her hands with qualities that heal: love, trust, faith, reconciliation, confession, sympathy, etc. Each person keeps his or her "healing hand" to use as part of this session's rite.

3. Mix the pieces of broken hearts, then let the group cooperatively reassemble the pieces to create a whole heart. When the hearts is whole again, glue the pieces to a white poster board background and pin to the wall as the central symbol of the rite.

4. Discuss the symbolism of the heart broken by sin and how the "healing hands" of love, faith, repentance, trust in God, reconciliation, etc., help to heal that heart.

Rite: Broken Heart

LEADER:
In the name of the Father, and of the Son, and of the Holy Spirit.

ALL:
Amen.

READER 1:
(Read Ezek 36:25-26.)

READER 2:
(Read Ps 51.)

ALL:
R. A clean heart create for me, O God.

READER 3:
(Read Jn 15:9-17.)

ALL:
(Pray the Confiteor from the Roman Missal:)

> I confess to almighty God,
> and to you my brothers and sisters,
> that I have sinned
>   through my own fault,
> in my thoughts and in my words,
> in what I have done,
> and in what I have failed to do.
> And I ask Blessed Mary ever Virgin,
> all the angels and saints,
> and you, my brothers and sisters,
> to pray for me to the Lord our God.

LEADER:
Let us now, as one family, exchange the sign of peace. (ALL *exchange the sign of peace.*) We are all wounded, all broken by sin. Yet we have faith that through acknowledgment of our sins, reconciliation, and God's love, our hearts may be made whole. As a token of that healing, let us walk forward and place the hands we have made around the symbol of the broken heart.

(*While each person walks forward and places his or her "hand of reconciliation" around the broken heart, all sing "Amazing Grace" or "I Hear of the Voice of Jesus Say" or any appropriate song of reconciliation.*)

ALL:
(*Pray the Rite of Penance:*)

> My God,
> I am sorry for my sins
>   with all my heart.
> In choosing to do wrong
> and failing to do good,
> I have sinned against you
> whom I should love above all things.
> I firmly intend, with your help,
> to do penance,
> to sin no more,
> and to avoid whatever leads me
>   to sin.
> Our Savior Jesus Christ
> suffered and died for us.
> In his name, my God, have mercy.

LEADER:
As a family, we have joined together to ask God to heal our hearts, which have been broken by sin. We trust in God that he will heal our wounds. May God, who has begun the good work in you, bring it to fulfillment.

ALL:
Amen.

(*Walking from person to person, LEADER sprinkles each participant with holy water by means of a fresh sprig of greenery. Each one then makes a sign of the cross as he or she feels the water. If desired, sing a concluding song.*)

(*If a priest is available, the sacrament of penance may be celebrated at this time.*)

12. I AM CHRIST'S HANDS AND FEET

Season or Occasion

- Lent

Purpose

- to offer a positive way to make sacrifices for Lent

Symbol

The symbol for this session is the Pilgrim Cross as the Wounded Christ, the Suffering Servant. As a friend of mine said when she saw this image: "My sins are the crown of thorns on Christ's head. Every time I sin, I dig it deeper into his forehead." This symbol enables us to *touch* Christ's wounds: to explore and ponder them in our own wounds. Yet Christ was not only wounded; he was the great healer.

Materials

- Using the Pilgrim Cross (also used in session 7, "True Vine") as the center, place four squares of purple felt at the four corners of the cross.
- Create and place a crown of thorns (either of real dried vegetation or a drawing) on the top square.
- Make flesh-colored felt hands and feet (drawing around your own is a short cut), place a scarlet cross in their centers, and place on the other three squares of felt.
- Cut out a red felt heart and affix it to the center of the cross.

Introduction

During World War II, a group of soldiers came across the burned-out rubble of a church. Nothing was left standing except a statue of Jesus with both hands blown off. Propped against the statue was a sign that said, "He had no hands but ours."

Used at the beginning of Lent, this session can provide "giving something up for Lent" with a deeper, long-term meaning.

Exercises

1. Have each person choose his or her favorite aspect of the symbol: Christ's wounded head, hands, feet, or heart. Ask the group members what they think the symbol means. What does it symbolize to them? How does the symbol embody this quotation from St. Teresa of Avila:

   Christ has no body now but yours.
   No hands, no feet on earth but yours.
   Yours are the eyes
       through which He looks,
   compassion on this world.
   Yours are the feet with which he walks
       to do good.
   He blesses all the world.

   Yours are the hands.
   Yours are the feet.
   Yours are the eyes.
   You are His body.

   Christ has no body now but yours.
   No hands, no feet on earth but yours.
   Yours are the eyes
       through which He looks,
   compassion on this world.
   Yours are the feet with which He walks
       to do good.
   Christ has no body now on earth
       but yours.

2. Read and discuss the following Scripture: Isaiah 42:1-4; Psalm 22:2-3,8-9,15-19; Isaiah 53:4-5.

3. Discuss instances when the participants felt abandoned and alone, helpless. Then discuss how each participant can become the Suffering Servant and Wounded Healer by "becoming" the part of Christ they chose. Being Christ's hands could be as simple as opening a door politely or as personal as sewing tiny clothes for the local hospital perinatal unit to clothe premature babies who have died. Being Christ's feet could mean entering a local charitable walk or race. Listening to someone in pain makes you Christ's ears. Volunteering for your local mental health and mental retardation center eases Christ's crown of thorns. Giving up that clever, critical remark at someone's expense makes you Christ's voice. Engaging in the sacrament of penance brings you closer to Christ's heart. The possibilities are endless.

4. While the group discusses these topics, have each person make a small, simple cross from twigs and yarn.

5. As an option for this session's rite, post the text of the "Anima Christi" and ask participants to copy the prayer onto index cards or other paper to use as a prayer text with their crosses.

Rite: I Am Christ's Hands and Feet

LEADER:

In the name of the Father, and of the Son, and of the Holy Spirit.

ALL:

Amen.

(While this traditional favorite of St. Ignatius Loyola, the "Anima Christi," is recited, each person walks forward, touches that part of Christ he or she chose, and silently consecrates himself or herself to become Christ's hands, feet, head, or heart during this Lenten season.)

LEADER:

(Recite the prayer as a litany, line by line.)

ALL:

(Respond after each line.) Lord, heal us.

> Soul of Christ, sanctify me.
> Body of Christ, heal me.
> Blood of Christ, inebriate me.
> Water from the side of Christ,
>   wash me.
> Passion of Christ, strengthen me.
>
> Good Jesus, hear me.

In your wounds shelter me.
From turning away keep me.
From the evil one protect me.
At the hour of my death call me.
Into your presence lead me,
to praise you with all your saints
for ever and ever.
Amen
(from *A Book of Prayers*).

LEADER:

(When all have completed the gesture of consecration and the litany, continue with:) Having consecrated ourselves to become the Suffering Servants of Christ, let us take up our crosses (ALL *pick up the twig crosses made earlier*) and begin our Lenten journey. Amen.

ALL:

(Sing "Lord, Who Throughout These Forty Days" or other appropriate Lenten hymn, or listen to John Michael Talbot's "Teresa's Song.")

(If your group meets after Easter, you may wish to share how the pledges were fulfilled.)

13. TENEBRAE/RESURRECTION

Season or Occasion

- Holy Week
- Easter
- passage from darkness to light

Purpose

- to emphasize the role that darkness, death, and resurrection play in our faith lives

Symbol

The symbol for this session again incorporates the Pilgrim Cross.

Materials

- the Lenten Pilgrim Cross (see session 7 or 12)
- Easter Pilgrim Cross (created for this session)
- a Christ candle to illuminate it
- nine candles in separate holders

Introduction

This session is based on the "Tenebrae" service. The Latin word *tenebrae* means "shadows" or "darkness." Prior to the 1950 restoration of the Holy Week liturgy, the Tenebrae service gave laity a means of participating in Holy Week, since pre-reform services were often held at odd times of the day with only clergy present. The Tenebrae-style service has been revived as a popular and moving prayer service using different formats, texts, and songs.

The original Tenebrae service was a combination of the ancient Offices of Matins and Lauds as recited during the Holy Week Triduum. It was distinguished by the gradual extinguishing of fifteen candles until only the central candle—the Christ candle—remained as a symbol of the promise of resurrection.

The rite in this session is an abbreviated version, adapting several elements of the traditional Tenebrae. It can take place in either a church chapel or any large bare space.

At the point in the rite where the sound of a tomb closing is called for, dragging a concrete block across another concrete block works well.

Exercises

1. Discuss:

   - Have you ever been in a place where the lights suddenly went out, plunging you into darkness?
   - Were you ever trapped somewhere, such as an elevator or subway? How did you and those with you feel in this situation? What action did you take and why?

2. Read and discuss Genesis 1:14-19 and John 1:1-5. These texts remind us that God will never allow us to remain in darkness.

   - How does our fear of darkness, isolation, entrapment, sin, and death affect our lives?

Rite: Tenebrae/Resurrection

(As the rite begins, the Lenten Pilgrim Cross is prominently displayed and is illuminated by the Christ candle. The other candles are placed at intervals around the space. They are freely accessible to the candle-acolytes, who extinguish them—one by one—after each reading.)

LEADER:
In the name of the Father, and of the Son, and of the Holy Spirit.

ALL:
Amen.

LEADER:
The story of salvation history is a struggle between darkness and light. Each of us has undergone that struggle in our own lives. Yet Christ our Light has suffered everything we have suffered. He understands our pain, our fear, our anger, and our dying. Let us walk with our forgiving Lord through the Valley of Death, for Christ has died, Christ has risen, Christ will come again.

Nocturn 1

READER 1:
(Read Ps 22:1-11,14,17-19.)

ALL:
R. My God, my God, why have you forsaken me?

(Candle 1 is extinguished.)

READER 2:
(Read Lam 3:1-9,14-18.)

ALL:
R. My soul is bereft of peace, I've forgotten what happiness is.

(Candle 2 is extinguished.)

READER 3:
(Read Ps 51:1-4,7-13,15-17.)

ALL:
R. Have mercy on me, O God, according to your steadfast love.

(Candle 3 is extinguished.)

ALL:
(Sing verse 1, "Were you there?")

Intercessions

(From "Good Friday Morning Prayer," Liturgy of the Hours, vol. 2.)

READER 4:
For our sake our Redeemer suffered death and was buried, and rose again. With heartfelt love let us adore him and pray.

ALL:
Lord, have mercy on us.

READER 4:
Christ, our teacher, for our sake you were obedient even to accepting death, teach us to obey the Father's will in all things.

ALL:
Lord, have mercy on us.

(ALL say the Lord's Prayer. Candle 4 is extinguished.)

Nocturn 2

READER 5:
(Read Ps 88:1-7,13-18.)

ALL:
R. O Lord, God of my salvation, at night I cry out in your presence.

(Candle 5 is extinguished.)

READER 6:
(Read Isa 53:2-5.)

ALL:
R. He was wounded for our transgressions, crushed for our iniquities.

(Candle 6 is extinguished.)

READER 7:
(Read Phil 2:5-11.)

ALL:
At the name of Jesus, every knee should bend.

(Candle 7 is extinguished.)

ALL:
(Sing verse 2, "Were you there?")

INTERCESSIONS

ALL:
Lord, have mercy on us.

READER 8:
Christ our salvation, you gave yourself up to death out of love for us, help us to show your love to one another.

ALL:
Lord, have mercy on us.

READER 8:
Christ our Savior, on the cross you embraced all time with your outstretched arms, unite God's scattered children in your kingdom of salvation.

ALL:
Lord, have mercy on us.

(ALL say the Lord's Prayer. Candle 8 is extinguished.)

Nocturn 3

ALL:
Lift high the Cross, the love of Christ proclaim, till all the world adore his sacred name.

(During the next reading, ALL may venerate the cross by walking forward and touching it.)

READER 9:
This is the wood of the cross on which is hung our salvation. The cross itself tells the story of its role in the crucifixion:

> Well I remember, a day in the
>   woodland,
> How I was hewed,
>   hacked from my trunk,
> Fierce fiends snatched and shaped
> me
> for a spectacle of shame to men;
> on their backs they bore me,
>   bade me stand,
> made me bear their beaten
> criminals.
> Standing I saw the Lord of love,
> Maker of man, hasten Himself,
> Come to the hill with courage high,
> Me He ascended, mighty and
> strong.
> The young Hero stripped Himself,
>   He who was mighty God,
> Stout and strong-hearted, He
> climbed
>   the towering Cross,
> With spirit manly,
>   for man He would save.
> I trembled as He touched me,
> cowered as He clasped me;
> Break down I dared not,
>   nor fall with fear.
> "Stand fast," my Lord commanded;
> A rood I was raised;
>   aloft I lifted the Lord,

King of high heaven;
  nor bend nor bow...
Hear and believe, my hero beloved,
That bitter woes I had to bear;
Hate and horror
  have happiness brought,
far and wide men pray,
  as they ought,
By this saving sign;
  redemption bought
By the Lord of heroes,
  on me was wrought.
For that am I splendid,
  high above heaven,
That I may heal my worshippers all.
The cruelest of gibbets
  once I was judged,
Hateful to men, but He, the Hero,
Opened by me the doors of life
("The Dream of the Rood,"
Anonymous, quoted in Mischke).

ALL:
Lift high the cross,
  the love of Christ proclaim,
till all the world adore his sacred name.

(Candle 9 is extinguished. The only candle left is Candle 10, the Christ candle, which illuminates the Lenten Pilgrim Cross. In silence, the candle is extinguished, leaving the space in total darkness. There is a sound resembling the closing of Christ's tomb. In the darkness, the Lenten Pilgrim Cross is removed or covered and the Easter Cross is set up or uncovered. After a suitable interval, the candle-acolytes relight the ten candles as well as those of the participants, and the Easter Cross is revealed.)

ALL:
(Sing "Christ the Lord Is Risen Today" or other appropriate song. If you have access to handbells, these may be rung.)

14. PENTECOST

Shepherd's crook courtesy of Keith Foegelle, Corpus Christi, Texas.

Season or Occasion

- Pentecost
- any retreat for those in ministry or for neophytes

Purpose

- to inspire, call, and send forth those engaged in ministry

Symbol

For this session, the Pilgrim Cross has a white felt dove on a red background above and felt feet wearing pilgrim's sandals below. Flesh-colored hands on a red felt background hold the Word and a shepherd's staff/crozier.

The red color and the white dove symbolize Pentecost: the birth of the church and the sending forth of the disciples. The sandaled feet and crozier symbolize discipleship: going forth to spread the Good News. The crozier is also the symbol of Christ as High Priest and of our own diocesan bishop, who is heir to St. Peter, the first bishop of Rome. Through the pope and our own bishop, we are empowered to go forth and minister.

Materials

- Pilgrim Cross (from session 7, 12, or 13)
- felt (red, white, flesh-colored, brown)
- glue
- Good Shepherd staff

68

Introduction

Pentecost is the birthday of the pilgrim church. It is also the pastoral feast of people in ministry: a time to call upon the Holy Spirit to inspire, to empower, and to send forth the people of God.

This session is for those active in ministry, for those concluding training who will be putting their theory into practice, or for neophytes about to launch themselves into the uncharted seas named "church."

Exercises

1. Read 1 Corinthians 3:1-17.

- Have you ever experienced the "jealousy and quarreling" that Paul mentions?
- How have you experienced the planting, watering, and growing process in your own life? In your ministry with others?
- How is Christ the foundation on which your life and ministry are built?

2. Ask the group what they think the symbol means.

- How does its symbolism relate to their personal faith journeys?

Rite: Pentecost

LEADER:
In the name of the Father, and of the Son, and of the Holy Spirit.

ALL:
Amen.

LEADER:
A reading from the first letter of Paul to the Corinthians. (*Read 1 Cor 12:3-7, 12-13*). The Word of the Lord.

ALL:
Thanks be to God.

(*Going around the group, each person says, "My name is N. My gift in the Spirit is.... After each gift is named, **ALL** respond: "Come Holy Spirit. Kindle in us the fire of your love." When finished, people may ask God for help in their ministry.*)

READER:
A reading from the Gospel of John. (*Read Jn 20:19-23.*)

LEADER:
Lord, you send our your Spirit and renew the face of the earth. May we use your gifts to minister wisely. For we are God's co-workers, God's field, and God's building. Let us go forth as your Pilgrim Church in Jesus Christ our Lord.

(*While **ALL** sing "Come Holy Ghost," each person goes to the **LEADER** to receive a blessing with the sign of the cross. **LEADER** lays hands on each person to send him or her forth.*)

15. ST. JOAN OF ARC

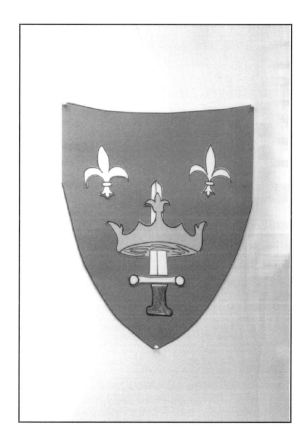

Season or Occasion

- Feast of St. Joan of Arc,
  Patron of Youth, May 30
- whenever strength against evil and sin
  is needed
- any youth occasion

Purpose

- to provide a strong, courageous role
  model for teens

Symbol

The symbol for St. Joan is her coat-of-arms,
given by King Charles when he raised her from
peasant status to the nobility. The gold crown
symbolizes the French monarchy as do the
gold *fleur-de-lis* on either side (*fleur-de-lis* also
symbolize the Virgin Mary). The crown can also
symbolize Christ the King, whom Joan served.
The silver-bladed sword with a gold hilt is part
of the knightly equipment Joan wore into battle.
It symbolizes the sword of justice and her
courage to fight for freedom in a world where
women had no legal rights or status. All the
symbols rest on a blue shield background.

Materials

- construction paper, poster board, or felt
  for Joan's coat-of-arms: blue background,
  gold crown and *fleur-de-lis*, silver-bladed
  sword with a gold hilt
- craft cord
- a small, inexpensive cross and Joan of
  Arc medal for each participant

Introduction

St. Joan of Arc (1412-1431) was an illiterate yet intelligent girl raised in France. Her country was occupied by English troops, torn by civil war, and crippled by a weak monarchy. Joan came from a good Catholic peasant family: hard-working, self-reliant, shrewd, and independent. One year, her home was burned to the ground by soldiers, so she was familiar with violence.

Around the age of thirteen, Joan began hearing heavenly voices and saw a vision of St. Michael the Archangel, St. Catherine, and St. Margaret. Over time, her voices insisted she must leave home, go to the French heir to the throne, Charles, and rally French troops to expel the English from France.

Overcoming ridicule, obstacles, and examinations by theologians, Joan was allowed to accompany the French army. Dressed in armor weighing more than fifty pounds, Joan inspired the military forces to win several victories. Always in the forefront of battle, she was wounded twice by arrows. When, as commanded by Joan's voices, Charles was at last crowned King of France, Joan stood at his side.

In May 1430, Joan was captured by the enemy during a battle. Abandoned by her French king and comrades, Joan was imprisoned, interrogated, brainwashed, and threatened with execution as a witch and heretic. Completely alone, Joan fought them with courage and humor. But after months of abuse, Joan recanted: she resumed women's dress and said her voices were only fantasies. Five days later, however, she again declared that God had sent her to free France and her voices were of divine origin.

On May 30, 1431, Joan was publicly burned at the stake and her ashes thrown into the river Seine. She was not yet twenty.

On July 7, 1456, the church declared her free of heresy and her trial and sentence false. On May 16, 1920, she was canonized.

Exercise

1. Read the above story of St. Joan of Arc. Discuss how her coat-of-arms symbolizes the armor to ward off evil (see Eph 6:10-18).

   - How is her story an inspiration and example for us?

2. Discuss in small groups:

   - Have you ever wanted to right a wrong but lacked the courage or support to take action?
   - Did you receive help from God and friends and family?

3. Read and discuss Ephesians 6:10-18.

   - How can the armor mentioned by St. Paul be translated into modern terms? (sword belt of truth, breastplate of righteousness, shield of faith, arrows of evil, helmet of salvation, sword of the Spirit).
   - Give specific examples of each (e.g., the shield of faith might be the Bible, which wards off the false messages of modern media).

Rite: St. Joan of Arc

LEADER:
In the name of the Father, and of the Son, and of the Holy Spirit.

ALL:
Amen.

LEADER:
We live in dangerous times. Violence and wrongdoing are everywhere. But the church gives us saints as role models to inspire us. Although St. Joan of Arc died more than five hundred years ago, she inspires us to fight evil for the sake of peace. Her story and this prayer service help us to arm ourselves in the fight against evil.

READER 1:
(Read Eph 6:11-18.)

READER 2:
(Read Isa 62:1-12.)

ALL:
(After every fourth verse and after the reading is finished:) R. You shall be a glorious crown in the hand of the Lord.

READER 3:
A reading from St. John Chrysostom, Father of the Church.

"I renounce you, Satan," you say. What has happened? What is this strange and unexpected turn of events? Did you rebel against your master—Satan? Did you look with scorn on his cruelty? Where comes this boldness of yours? "I have a strong weapon," you say. What weapon? What ally? Tell me! "I enter in your service, O Christ," you reply. "Therefore, I'm bold and rebel against Satan, for I have a strong place of refuge. Although I was trembling and afraid before, now I renounce him."

Let us therefore take courage and strip ourselves for the contests. Christ has put on us armor that is more glittering than any gold, stronger than any steel, hotter and more violent than any fire, and lighter than any breath of air. The nature of this armor does not burden and bend our knees, but it gives wings to our limbs and lifts them all up. If you wish to take flight to heaven, this armor is no hindrance. It is a new kind of armor, since it is a new kind of combat.

Although I am human, I must aim my blows at demons; although clad in flesh, my struggle is with incorporeal powers. On this account, God has made my breastplate not from metal but from justice; God has prepared for me a shield which is made not of bronze but of faith. I have, too, a sharp sword, the word of the Spirit *(Easter Sourcebook* 124-5).

LEADER:
(After each formulary [taken from the Rite of Baptism for Children*] is read,* **ALL** *respond: "I do.")*

Do you reject sin so as to live in the freedom of God's children?

Do you reject the glamor of evil, and refuse to be mastered by sin?

Do you reject Satan, father of sin
and prince of darkness?

Do you reject Satan, and all his
works, and all his empty promises?

LEADER:
St. Joan of Arc lived during the Middle
Ages. She dressed as a knight in her battle
for peace and justice. A knight of the
Middle Ages went through a ceremony
where he knelt before the king he served,
placed his hands between the king's, and
swore to be faithful to him. We will now
go through the same ceremony, pledging
our allegiance and loyalty to Christ the
King.

*(This ceremony may take place in silence
or with soft music playing. LEADER is
seated. Each participant walks forward,
kneels, and places his or her hands
between leader's hands. LEADER speaks
each person's name as he or she comes
forward.)*

LEADER:
N., do you pledge allegiance and loyalty to
Christ the King?

PARTICIPANT:
*(Kneeling, with both hands between the
leader's)* I do.

LEADER:
May God, who has begun the good work
in you, bring it to fulfillment. In the name of
the Father, and of the Son, and of the Holy
Spirit. *(Make sign of the cross on the
participant's forehead. Place necklace
consisting of a small cross and a medal of
St. Joan of Arc around the participant's
neck. At the conclusion of the ceremony,
continue:)* Putting on the armor of God and
holding our faith as a shield, let us now go
forward and fight the good fight, just as
Joan or Arc did.

ALL:
Amen.

*(If desired, an appropriately rousing song
may conclude the rite.)*

16. TRIUMPH OF THE CROSS

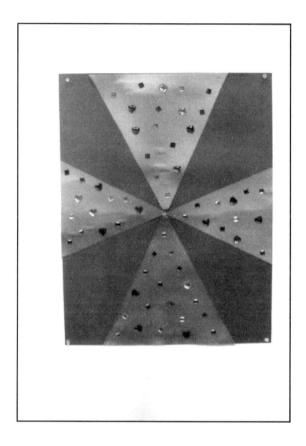

Season or Occasion

- Feast of the Triumph of the Cross, September 14

Purpose

- to embrace, honor and glorify the cross as an integral part of our faith as Catholics

Symbol

The symbol for this session is the Cross of Glory, symbolic of Christ transfigured.

Materials

- a large wall cross, wooden or cardboard
- gold paint
- acrylic craft jewels
- glue
- popsicle sticks or cardboard for mini-crosses
- yarn for mini-crosses

Introduction

While people automatically associate crucifixes with Catholicism, early Christians would have reacted in horror to a crucifix in a worship space. Crucifixion was a shameful death reserved for the lowest criminals, just as the electric chair is now. The image of the cross was not widely used in Christian art until the fourth century, and the crucifix did not became common until the thirteenth century.

When the cross finally began to be used in churches, it was the cross of glory, made of gold, studded with gems, and set in a starry sky. Christ's body did not hang on this cross. In the churches of Santa Pudenziana, Rome (402-417), and Sant' Apollinare in Classe (c. 549), fabulous glittering wall mosaics depicted jeweled crosses above their altars. Set among ninety-nine stars, the cross of Sant' Apollinare in Classe symbolized the mysterious transformation of the bread and wine into Eucharist, which took place on the altar directly below it.

Distaste for the cross is alive and well in our own time, in which people regard suffering and dying to self as "negative," "depressing," and "masochistic." But as Christ taught, only through dying are we born to new life. "What you sow does not come to life unless it dies" (1 Cor 15:36). This is why we venerate the cross on Good Friday, a custom originating in Jerusalem in the fifth century. Flanked by two deacons, the bishop of Jerusalem would hold a relic of the true cross for the devout to kiss. (A story is told how the deacons were more than merely ornamental. One year a worshiper walked up to the true cross and bit a chunk out of it as a souvenir! After that, the deacons also served as bodyguards.)

Tradition holds that St. Helena gave her son Constantine one of the nails of the true cross. When he erected an equestrian statue of himself in Constantinople, the Emperor Constantine used the nail from the true cross as a bit between the teeth of the bronze horse his effigy rode. He did not let his imperial power blind him to the real power that governed the world.

In preparation for this session's rite, you may wish to rehearse certain participants ahead of time in mime-action to accompany the reading of "The Dream of the Rood."

Exercises

1. While a real wooden cross would be ideal, you can make a cross from cardboard, spray-paint it gold, and glue on acrylic "jewels" from the craft store (flat on one side and faceted jewel-like on the other.) For the rite, you will need mini-crosses made from popsicle sticks or cardboard, sprayed gold, with a single craft jewel glued on. Tie a yarn loop on it to hang around the neck.

2. Read and discuss this quotation from St. Augustine:

That Cross which was the derision of His enemies is now displayed on the forehead of kings. The effect has proven His power; He conquered the world, not by the word, but by the wood. The wood of the Cross was thought a thing of scorn by His enemies, who stood before it and wagged their heads, shouting: "If He is the Son of God, let Him come down from that Cross."

• How do I avoid the cross in my own life?
• How can I better embrace it as a Catholic?
• How can I help others who struggle to carry their own crosses?

Rite: Triumph of the Cross

(The Cross of Glory hangs on a centrally located wall in the worship space and is flanked by candles.)

LEADER:
In the name of the Father, and of the Son, and of the Holy Spirit.

ALL:
Amen.

LEADER:
May I never boast of anything except the cross of our Lord Jesus Christ, by which the world has been crucified to me, and I to the world (Gal 6:14).

ALL:
Alleluia!

READER 1:

> How splendid the Cross of Christ!
> It brings life, not death;
> light, not darkness;
> Paradise, not its loss.
> It is the wood on which the Lord,
> like a great warrior,
> was wounded in hands and feet
>   and side,
> but healed thereby our wounds.
> A tree had destroyed us,
> A tree now brought us life
> (Theodore of Studios).

READER 2:
In the eighth century, an anonymous Anglo-Saxon poet wrote a poem called "The Dream of the Rood" ("rood" is an Old English term which refers to the true cross). In this poem, the cross itself speaks, telling the story of how it is transformed from a tree into an instrument of salvation.

Well I remember,
  a day in the woodland,
How I was hewed,
  hacked from my trunk,
Fierce fiends snatched and shaped me
for a spectacle of shame to men;
on their backs they bore me,
  bade me stand,
made me bear their beaten criminals.
Standing I saw the Lord of love,
Maker of man, hasten Himself,
Come to the hill with courage high,
Me He ascended, mighty and strong.
The young Hero stripped Himself,
  He who was mighty God,
Stout and strong-hearted,
  He climbed the towering Cross,
With spirit manly,
  for man He would save.
I trembled as He touched me,
cowered as He clasped me;
Break down I dared not,
  nor fall with fear.
"Stand fast," my Lord commanded;
A rood I was raised;
  aloft I lifted the Lord,
King of high heaven;
  nor bend nor bow....
Hear and believe, my hero beloved,
That bitter woes I had to bear;
Hate and horror
  have happiness brought,
far and wide men pray, as they ought,
By this saving sign,
  redemption bought.
By the Lord of heroes,

on me was wrought.
For that am I splendid,
   high above heaven,
That I may heal my worshippers all.
The cruelest of gibbets
   once I was judged,
Hateful to men, but He, the Hero,
Opened by me the doors of life.
Then I gleamed golden in every
part:
the Tree of the World
outstretched to its four corners.
Where I touched the heavens
   and earth, gems glowed.
And at my heart,
   where the two beams met,
five precious jewels
   shone most gloriously.
Heaven's multitudes,
   the hosts of angels
worshipped the Cross.
They gazed upon me,
   created for glory
   before time began.
Truly, I tell you, I am no gallows
tree.
The Cross is the glory
   of the heavenly powers,
of all the nations of the earth,
and of the whole creation
("The Dream of the Rood,"
Anonymous, quoted in Mischke).

ALL:
(Stand, divide into partners, and face one another. Sign each other with the sign of the cross according to the following directives.)

LEADER:
Let us now embrace the power of
the cross of Christ, who triumphed
over sin and death:

Receive the cross on your forehead:
   It is Christ himself who now
   strengthens you with this sign
   of his love.
Receive the sign of the cross
   on your ears, that you may hear
   the voice of the Lord.
Receive the sign of the cross
   on your eyes, that you may see
   the glory of God.
Receive the sign of the cross
   on your lips, that you may
   respond to the word of God.
Receive the sign of the cross
   over your heart, that Christ may
   dwell there by faith.
Receive the sign of the cross
   on your shoulders, that you may
   bear the gentle yoke of Christ.
Receive the sign of the cross
   on your hands, that Christ may be
   known in the work which you do.
Receive the sign of the cross
   on your feet, that you may walk
   in the way of Christ
("Rite of Acceptance into the Order
of Catechumens," *Rite of Christian
Initiation of Adults* 55-6).

LEADER:

God stretched forth his hands
upon the Cross to embrace the
utmost limits of the earth
(St. Cyril of Jerusalem).

Let us follow his example as we honor the
cross on which hung our salvation.

ALL:
*(Walk forward to face the Cross of Glory on
the wall, stop, and lift arms shoulder-high,
palms up, as living crosses. Bow to the
Cross of Glory and receive a mini-cross
around the neck before returning to your*

seats. While this is taking place, sing: "Were You There?")

LEADER:

Almighty God,
by the cross and resurrection
  of your Son,
you have given life to your people.

Your servants have received
  the sign of the cross;
make them living proof
of its saving power
and help them to persevere
  in the footsteps of Christ
("Rite of Acceptance into the Order
of Catechumens," *Rite of Christian
Initiation of Adults* 57).

ALL:
We adore you, O Christ, and we praise
you, because by your cross, you have
redeemed the world. Amen. (*Sing "Lift
High the Cross."*)

17. ANGELS

Angel image courtesy of Jamie Aven, San Antonio, Texas.

Season or Occasion

- Feast of the Guardian Angel, October 2
- Feast of the Holy Archangels, September 29

Purpose

- to provide a Catholic study of angels based on tradition and Scripture rather than on secular or New Age culture

Symbol

The central symbol for this exercise is a large image of an angel.

Materials

- white, gold, and red felt
- glue
- long corsage pins
- fluffy white material
- paper for "angel scrolls"
- gold ribbon
- felt-tip pens or crayons
- bowl

Introduction

Angels are everywhere these days. Unfortunately, they're seen mostly on secular media and merchandise. They flit across T-shirts, dangle as jewelry, glow as candles, perch coyly atop planters and flap across TV screens to the narration of well-known actresses.

Gift catalogs offer angel books that guarantee the reader will align himself or herself with the "angelic energy field" for guidance in love, commerce, and healing. (In partnership with Zoltan the astrologer, no doubt.)

The ironic thing about this end-of-the-millennium malarkey is that while secular angel advocates abound in our culture, Catholic interest in angels waned to the point of extinction after Vatican II.

Yet Catholic belief in angels goes back to the very beginnings of the church. The *Catechism of the Catholic Church* says that "the existence of the spiritual, non-corporeal beings that sacred Scripture calls 'angels' is a truth of faith. The witness of Scripture is as clear as the unanimity of Tradition" (328).

The early church fathers and saints also speak of angels:

> We should pray to angels, for they are given us as guardians (St. Ambrose).

> So valuable to heaven is the dignity of the human soul that every member of the human race has a guardian angel from the moment the person begins to be (St. Jerome).

> Beside each believer stands an angel as protector and shepherd leading him to life (St. Basil).

> Make yourself familiar with the angels, and behold them frequently in spirit; for without being seen, they are present with you (St. Frances de Sales.)

> I say of the Angels—every breath of air and ray of light and heat, every beautiful prospect is, as it were, the skirts of their garments, the waving robes of those whose faces see God (Cardinal John Henry Newman).

Exercises

1. If your group is artistically inclined, you can create your own angel symbol. If not, you can use one of the many posters or calendars of angels available on the commercial market. My angel was created by San Antonio artist Jamie Aven, whose images of the Virgin Mary and Good Shepherd also appear in this book. Beneath the angel arrange a white, fluffy, cloud-like piece of material. The "angel scrolls" will be placed on this. Create felt "angel wings" with a heart in the center for each participant, or have participants make their own. Pin extra angel wings all around the central image of the angel, using big pearl-headed corsage pins. Place the wings for participants in a bowl.

2. Have each participant draw a picture of an occasion when they were "touched by an angel"—when God sent someone to help or guard them in time of need. A symbol of the occasion is sufficient: a car if someone changed a flat tire, a medical symbol for a medical emergency, etc. On the back, have each participant draw a symbol of how he or she is a ministering angel to others: a sneaker if they participate in charitable walk-a-thons, food if they bring meals-on-wheels, a book if they teach, etc. Discuss these occasions in small groups.

Then roll the drawings into scrolls and tie with gold ribbons.

2. Read the following quotation by St. Bernard of Clairvaux. Discuss how it reflects our belief in God's compassionate care. What impact should it have on our lives and ministries?

He has given his Angels charge of you to guard you in all your ways. How this ought to produce respect in you, to promote devotion and to provide confidence! Respect because of the presence of the Angels, devotion because of their friendliness, and confidence because of their guardianship. His angels are everywhere: in every nook and cranny. Respect your angel. They are present not only with you, but even for you. To protect for you and benefit you. What shall you repay to the lord for all he has given you?....

Consider, dearest brethren, how careful we ought to be to show ourselves worthy of such noble company and so to live in the sight of the holy angels that they shall see nothing in our conduct to displease them....If, then, we find the companionship of the angels so necessary for us, we ought carefully to avoid anything that could displease them and to cultivate those virtues especially in which they take particular delight.... such as sobriety, chastity, voluntary poverty, frequent ejaculations to God, prayers offered up with contrite tears and a pure intention of heart.

But above and beyond all these, unity and peace the "angels of peace" demand from us. We ought to think and speak alike and have no divisions amongst us, but rather to show that we are all, collectively, one body in Christ and members individually one of another.

3. If your gathering includes food, you might ask participants to bring "angel" food for fun: angel food cake, angel hair pasta, etc. Or, conversely, they might bring devil's food cake and deviled eggs!

Rite: Angels

LEADER:

The name "angel" is the Greek translation of a Hebrew word meaning "messenger." Angels are an integral part of God's saving plan, as the Letter to the Hebrews states:

> Are not all angels spirits in the divine service, sent to serve for the sake of those who are to enherit salvation? (1:14).

Let us listen to the Word of God for it assures us that God sends angels to protect us from all evil.

READER 1:

(Read 1 Kings:3-8.)

READER 2:

(Read Ps 34:1-9.)

ALL:

R. Happy are those that take refuge in God.

READER 3:

(Read Mt 18:10-14.)

LEADER:

Let us offer our petitions to God, secure in the knowledge that he will send his angels to watch over us and our needs. *(Read previously prepared intentions and invite ALL to offer spontaneous petitions as well, for themselves and for others.)*

ALL:

(Sing "On Eagle's Wings." One by one, walk forward and place "angel scroll" beneath the angel image. After all have returned to their places, pass the bowl of angel wings around. Let each person pin angel wings on his or her neighbor and exchange a sign of peace.)

LEADER:

For centuries, Catholics have believed that God sends his angels to guard and to guide us. As we conclude this prayer service, let us join hands and bow our heads as we ask God to send his angels to protect us. *(Read Ex 23:20-23.)*

ALL: Amen.

18. ST. FRANCIS OF ASSISI

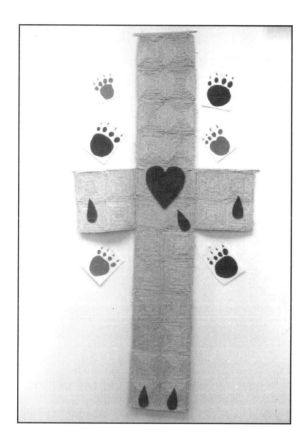

Season or Occasion

- Feast of St. Francis of Assisi, October 4

Purpose

- to honor St. Francis of Assisi's love of all living things as creatures of God

Symbol

The symbol of St. Francis is the cross bearing the marks of the stigmata, which he received in a vision. Because the Franciscan habit is brown and made of the simple materials suitable to a life of poverty, the pictured cross was made from squares of coarse, dried, woven natural grasses. The stigmata and heart are made of red felt. Surrounding the St. Francis Cross are "pawprints" made by participants from multicolored construction paper.

Materials

- squares of natural fiber floor matting or any other natural, simple material for the cross
- red felt for stigmata
- construction paper for pawprints
- scissors
- glue

Introduction

Although he died more than seven hundred years ago, almost everyone—Catholic or not—has heard of St. Francis of Assisi (1181-1226). Like Mother Teresa of Calcutta, he has become a universal symbol of gentleness and respect for all living things. Born into the wealthy merchant class, Francis lived a care-free youth, going to parties and to war with equal hilarity. His life was totally reversed, however, when he saw a vision of Christ. After making a pilgrimage to Rome, Francis totally changed his life. Selling some of his merchant father's silk to care for the poor, he was publicly disinherited.

Francis embraced a life dedicated to Lady Poverty and preaching, founding the Franciscan Order in 1206. Yet Francis was far from a "Gloomy Gus." He sang and danced, played imaginary fiddles, and spun a follower in circles to determine which fork of the road to take. He created the first live Christmas creche in 1223 (it was hard to follow the service over the donkey's braying, but everybody voted it worthwhile). The book *The Little Flowers of St. Francis* is filled with stories of Francis kissing lepers, taming a wolf, buying and building a nest for tame doves, and converting robbers. While praying in his cell in 1224, he received the stigmata, the wounds of Christ. Francis was canonized two years after his death.

Exercises

1. Read and discuss "Canticle of the Sun" by St. Francis:

   Most High, omnipotent, good Lord
   To you alone belong praise and glory,
   honor and blessing.
   No man is worthy to breathe thy name.

   Be praised, my Lord, for all your
   creatures.

   In the first place for the blessed Brother
   Sun,
   who gives us the day and enlightens us
   through you.
   He is beautiful and radiant
   with his great splendor.
   Giving witness of thee,
   Most Omnipotent One.

   Be praised, my Lord, for Sister Moon
   and the starts
   formed by you so bright, precious
   and beautiful.

   Be praised my Lord, for Brother Wind
   and the airy skies, so cloudy and serene;

   for every weather, be praised,
   for it is life-giving.

   Be praised, my Lord, for Sister Water,
   so necessary yet so humble, precious,
   and chaste.

   Be praised, my Lord, for Brother Fire,
   who lights up the night.
   He is beautiful and carefree, robust
   and fierce.

   Be praised, my Lord, for our sister,
   Mother Earth,
   who nourishes and watches us
   while bringing forth abundance of fruits
   with colored flowers and herbs.

   Be praised, my Lord, for those who
   pardon
   through your love
   and bear weakness and trial.
   Blessed are those who endure in peace,
   for they will be crowned by you, Most
   High.

Be praised, my Lord, for our sister,
  Bodily Death,
whom no living man can escape.
Woe to those who die in sin.
Blessed are those who discover
  thy holy will
the second death will do them no harm.

Praise and bless my Lord.
Render thanks.
Serve him with great humility. Amen.

2. Discuss

- How does St. Francis' life, dedicated to cherishing all creation, inspire us to do the same?
- What is the position of the Catholic church on respecting all nature and all life?
- How can we follow the example of St. Francis in our daily lives?

3. Have each participant think of a special pet or favorite animal species they wish to place under the care of St. Francis. Make a construction paper "pawprint" and write that animal or a related slogan or theme ("Save the whales") on it.

Rite: St. Francis of Assisi

LEADER:
In the name of the Father, and of the Son, and of the Holy Spirit.

ALL:
Amen.

LEADER:
Wonderful are all God's works. Blessed be the name of the Lord.

ALL:
Now and forever.

READER 1:
(Read Gen 1:20-25.)

READER 2:
(Read Ps 148:1,3-5,7-14.)

ALL:
R. Praise the name of the Lord. His name is exalted.

NARRATOR:
Let us now listen to the story of how St. Francis tamed the wolf.

One day, St. Francis visited the city of Gubbio while it was being terrorized by a fierce, wild wolf. The wolf was so ferocious that it not only ate animals, it ate humans as well. Every time the townspeople went into the surrounding countryside, they carried weapons as if going to war. But even their weapons couldn't beat off this ferocious wolf. Most of them refused to go out of town at all.

ST. FRANCIS:
The countryside is so beautiful today. I believe I'll go for a walk.

TOWNSPERSON:
Francis, don't go outside! That terrible wolf will eat you up!

ST. FRANCIS:
But no one has gone outside the city walls for days! You can't go on living like this! I'm going to talk some sense into that wolf. God will protect me. (Makes the sign of the cross and goes to meet the wolf, despite the frightened pleading of the townspeople.)

NARRATOR:
Protected, not by a sword or shield, but by the sign of the cross, St. Francis bravely went out to meet the wolf.

(FRANCIS and TOWNSPERSON walk a little way. Then the frightened TOWNSPERSON stops and refuses to go farther.)

TOWNSPERSON:
(Fearfully) Francis, I don't want to let you down, but I'm afraid to go any farther. The wolf might hurt me!

ST. FRANCIS:
Stay here, then. But I want to meet this monster that everybody's been talking about.

(WOLF darts out furiously from its hiding place, snarling at FRANCIS. The TOWNSPERSON yelps and throws himself flat on the floor, burying his head in his arms. FRANCIS bravely holds his ground and makes the sign of the cross over WOLF, who skids to a halt.)

TOWNSPERSON:
(Still hiding eyes) Don't eat me, Mr. Wolf! Please don't eat me! Eat the monk! Eat Brother Francis!

ST. FRANCIS:
Come to me, Brother Wolf. In the name of Christ, I order you not to hurt me or anyone in this region.

(WOLF *quietly lies down at Francis's feet. TOWNSPERSON peeks at the wolf, moans, plays possum.*)

TOWNSPERSON:
(*Whispering*) If I lie perfectly still, maybe the wolf will think I'm dead and go away.

ST. FRANCIS:
Brother Wolf, you've terrorized the townspeople of Gubbio. You've destroyed animals and humans for miles around. The whole town is your enemy. The town is ready to send its bravest warriors against you!

TOWNSPERSON:
(*Trembling, eyes still shut*) Mercy, Mr. Wolf! Mercy!

ST. FRANCIS:
I want to make peace between you and the townspeople, so they will forgive the crimes you committed against them. Do you ask forgiveness for the people and animals you've killed without mercy?

(WOLF *nods and makes dog noises and gestures, begging forgiveness from FRANCIS.*)

ST. FRANCIS:
(To TOWNSPERSON) My brother, will you pardon the wolf in the name of your town?

TOWNSPERSON:
(*After some encouragement, timidly rises and nods agreement*) Yes, Brother Francis. I will pardon the wolf. (*Bravely*) Good doggy!

ST. FRANCIS:
Then both of you exchange the kiss of peace.

(TOWNSPERSON *does so fearfully; WOLF does it eagerly, like a boisterous puppy.*)

ST. FRANCIS:
Brother Wolf, since you are willing to keep the peace, I promise the townspeople will give you food everyday. I know the evil you've done was because of hunger. (*To* TOWNSPERSON) My brother, do you promise to keep the wolf fed from now on?

TOWNSPERSON:
(*Arrogantly*) Well, I don't know about that! It's all very well for you monks to talk, but we businessmen have to make a living! (*Takes out paper and pencil and begins to jot down figures*) Say we feed the wolf five pounds of horse meat a day—that's a gold piece a week—times fifty-two weeks per year, that's—

(WOLF *growls gently and nips at Townsperson's leg.*)

TOWNSPERSON:
(*Jumps back and drops paper and pencil*) That's cheap at the price! Very reasonable! Couldn't have made a better deal myself! Brother Francis, you should have been a diplomat. (*Sidles cautiously away from* WOLF *and runs out of sight.*)

ST. FRANCIS:
Brother Wolf, now that I've done this favor for you, I want a favor in return. Will you promise never to hurt anyone here again? (WOLF *nods and whimpers.*) Give me a pledge so I can believe what you promise. (WOLF *gives* FRANCIS *his paw and* FRANCIS *pets* WOLF.)

NARRATOR:
From that day on, the wolf and the townspeople kept the pact that St. Francis made. When the wolf went from door to door, the people fed it faithfully, and even the town dogs refused to bark at it. And

when the wolf grew old and died, the people were sorry because its peacefulness reminded them of the virtues and holiness of St. Francis of Assisi.

LEADER:
(Reads the intercessions, adapted from "Order for the Blessing of Animals," Book of Blessings.) God created us and placed us on this earth to be the stewards of all living things and so to proclaim the glory of their Creator. Let us, then, praise God, saying:

ALL:
How great are the works of your hands, Lord.

LEADER:
We praise you, Lord, who created the animals and gave us the ability to train them to help us in our work.

ALL:
How great are the works of your hands, Lord.

LEADER:
We praise you, Lord, who give us domestic animals as companions.

ALL:
How great are the works of your hands, Lord.

LEADER:
We praise you, Lord, who show us a sign of your providence, as Jesus told us, by caring for the birds of the air.

ALL:
How great are the works of your hands, Lord.

LEADER:
We praise you, Lord, who offered your Son as the Paschal Lamb. In him you willed that we should be called and should truly be your children.

ALL:
How great are the works of your hands, Lord.

LEADER:
We praise you, Lord, who through your lowliest creatures never cease to draw us toward your love.

ALL:
How great are the works of your hands, Lord.

LEADER:
(Ask for spontaneous intercessions.)

ALL:
(When the intercessions are concluded, sing "Make me a Channel of your Peace" while each participant walks forward and fastens his or her pawprint symbol around the St. Francis Cross on the wall.)

LEADER:

Hear our humble prayer, O God,
for our friends the animals,
    your creatures.
We pray especially for all that
    are suffering in any way:
for the overworked and underfed,
the hunted, lost, or hungry;
for all in captivity or ill-treated,
and for those that must be put
    to death.

For those who deal with them
we ask a heart of compassion,
    gentle hands, and kindly words.
Make us all true friends to animals
and worthy followers
    of our merciful Savior, Jesus Christ
("Other Prayers for Animals," Catholic Household Blessings and Prayers).

ALL:
Amen. *(Sing "All things Bright and Beautiful.")*

19. ALL SOULS/ALTARCITOS

Season or Occasion

- All Souls Day
- Remembering the dead
- Hispanic *Altarcitos*

Purpose

- to allow participants to create their own personal memorial of a loved one on All Souls' Day or on the anniversary of a death

Symbol

The symbol for this session is an altarcito to be created by the participants with personal mementos of their deceased loved ones.

Materials

- Call participants ahead of time and ask them to bring mementos or belongings that clearly recall a deceased loved one: books, photos, songs, Scripture verses, religious belongings such as rosaries or holy pictures, a favorite perfume, a favorite food, tools used in a hobby, objects symbolizing the work they engaged in, a favorite flower, etc. Anything goes; try to engage all the senses with these mementos: sight, sound, smell, taste, touch.
- a bowl full of flowers (ideally a favorite of one of the deceased). Participants will place these flowers on the *altarcito* during this session's rite.
- candles to place on the *altarcito*

Introduction

The Feast of All Souls, the Mexican Day of the Dead, is time devoted to telling stories of the beloved dead. Traditionally, the Day of the Dead is celebrated by gathering at family graves to clean and decorate them. However, this session approaches the topic through another Hispanic custom: the *altarcito*, a tiny altar or prayer corner.

The "altarcito" pictured on the previous page belonged to Guadalupe Moreno Fernandez, the mother of my friend Elsa Guajardo. Although Mrs. Fernandez died in May 1992, the tiny *nicho* (niche) she left behind calls up vivid memories for her family.

"We grew up having devotions and sacramentals," explains Elsa, fingering the tiny objects. "St. Anthony—my mother said a chaplet to him every Tuesday." Her father, Nicholas G. Fernandez, always used a glass jar of holy water to bless himself each time he left the house.

Such customs were never mere outward piety—all show and no effort. "As a member of the Blue Army, my mother was inspired to buy this statue of Our Lady of Fatima and have the niche made. During the first nine days of each month, she took this pilgrim statue to the house of anyone who wanted it and said the rosary. Especially in May and October." A votive candle burned inside the *nicho* everyday, all day.

A prayer card of San Ramon Nonato invokes a story close to Elsa's heart. "When I was born, Mother almost lost me. Her sister sat at her side during the two-day labor and said, 'Sistita, why don't you pray to San Ramon for help?'" So Elsa's mother offered her up to the saint and named her Ramona Elsa Iña.

The memories invoked by the *altarcito* encompass many generations. A picture of the Santo Niño de Atocha belonged to Elsa's grandmother. Snapshots document the different generations. Just as Elsa's mother prayed daily for her children, so Elsa prays for her own. A red ribbon saying "Hugs, not Drugs" is Elsa's request for God's protection. "My daughters Laura, Elsa Anne, and Marie Therese also have their devotions," she adds.

Even death is benignly present in the *altarcito*. A dried flower from Mrs. Fernandez's coffin lies inside, as well as her corsage worn during the last family reunion she attended. On the table stands a favorite reproduction of Michelangelo's *Pieta*, which is also at the grave of Elsa's parents. "We pray for those who have preceded us in death and have faith they have joined the saints in heaven," says Elsa. "When my mother was alive, I took her to the cemetery for Mass and the blessing of the graves every November 2. Now both parents are there, I continue the tradition. All our Catholic family traditions, past and present, interweave." (Elsa's immediate family also includes her children Bill, Jerry, Mary, Paul, Nick, Fred, and her husband of more than thirty years, Guillermo "Willie" Guajardo. Marvin, the cat, is adopted.)

Traditional Hispanic-American culture does not segregate the living and the dead as stringently as modern mainstream American culture does. Through traditional customs of the Hispanic-American culture, this session encourages exploration of the emotions we associate with the dead.

Exercises

1. Discuss the objects participants brought to create the group *altarcito*.

- How do these objects recall the deceased (a favorite medal worn as a parish member of the Guadalupanas, a rosary always seen in their hands, a photo of a special family occasion, etc.)?

2. Tell old stories and jokes previously shared with loved ones now deceased. Laugh, cry, recall the blessings as well as the sorrows.

- How does this process help us grieve?
- How does it keep the memory of the deceased alive?
- How does it help us continue to live with courage, hope, and faith?

Rite: All Souls/Altarcitos

(Texts are derived from "Morning Prayer" and "Evening Prayer," *Order of Christian Funerals*.)

LEADER:
(Welcome ALL and explain how they have gathered together to honor and remember their loved ones as symbolized by the altarcito. Add how the deceased enriched their lives and in what way. Ask previously designated participants to light the candles in the altarcito.)

Let us therefore begin this rite of remembrance together. God, come to my assistance.

ALL:
Lord, make haste to help me.

LEADER:
Glory to the Father, and to the Son, and to the Holy Spirit.

ALL:
As it was in the beginning, is now, and will be forever. Amen.

READER 1:
(Read Ps 121.)

ALL:
R. The Lord will keep you from all evil; he will guard your soul.

READER 2:
(Read 1 Thess 4:13-18.)

LEADER:
(Use the following intercessions and/or ask for spontaneous intercessions from ALL.)
Let us pray to the all-powerful Father, who raised Jesus from the dead and gives new life to our mortal bodies, and say to him:

ALL:
Lord, give us new life in Christ.

LEADER:
Father, through baptism we have been buried with your Son and have risen with him in his resurrection. Grant that we may walk with newness of life so that when we die, we may live with Christ forever.

ALL:
Lord, give us new life in Christ.

LEADER:
Christ, consoler of those who mourn, you dried the tears of the family of Lazarus, of the widow's son, and of the daughter of Jairus. Comfort those who mourn for the dead.

ALL:
Lord, give us new life in Christ.

LEADER:
Lord, when at last our earthly home is dissolved, give us a home, not of earthly making but built of eternity in heaven.

ALL:
Lord, give us new life in Christ. *(Read the Magnificat, Lk 1:47-55. Then walk forward and place flowers on the* altarcito *while* LEADER *reads the following.)*

LEADER:
May the angels lead you into paradise;
may the martyrs come to welcome you
and take you to the Holy City,
the new and eternal Jerusalem.

ALL:
May the angels lead you into paradise;
may the martyrs come to welcome you

and take you to the Holy City,
the new and eternal Jerusalem.

LEADER:
May the choirs of angels welcome you
and lead you to the bosom of Abraham;
where Lazarus is poor no longer
may you find eternal rest.

ALL:
May you find eternal rest.

LEADER:
With God there is mercy and fullness of
redemption; let us pray as Christ taught us.

ALL:
Our Father...

LEADER:
Lord, as we remember N., we turn to you.
Are you not the God of love who opens
your ears to all? Listen to our prayers for
your servant, N., whom you have
numbered among your own people. Lead
him/her to your kingdom of light and
peace and count him/her among the
saints in glory.

We ask this through our Lord Jesus Christ,
your Son, who lives and reigns with you
and the Holy Spirit, One God, for ever and
ever.

ALL:
Amen. (*Sing "For All the Saints."*)

20. ALL SAINTS

Season or Occasion

- Feast of All Saints

Purpose

- to demonstrate how we are all called to be saints

Symbol

A doll-sized "portrait" of each participant is taped to the wall after the session is completed to symbolize the communion of saints.

Materials

- white poster board
- crayons
- scissors
- tape
- If you have a large group, call people ahead of time and ask them to bring their own supplies.

Introduction

We are all called to be saints. There are as many roads to sainthood as there are people canonized. Martyrdom isn't necessarily a requirement, for as St. Teresa of Avila noted, "The Lord walks among the pots and pans," and Therese of the Little Flower said, "Pick up a pin for the love of God and perhaps you can save a soul." One fun song that sums it all up is the hymn "I Sing a Song of the Saints of God," which lists the innumerable ways to heaven (a member of my choir used to call this British hymn the "fierce wild beast song"):

> I sing a song of the saints of God,
> patient and brave and true,
> who toiled and fought and lived and died
> for the Lord they loved and knew.
> And one was a doctor,
>   and one was a queen,
> and one was a shepherdess
>   on the green:
> they were all of them saints of God—
> and I mean, God helping, to be one too.
>
> They loved their Lord so dear, so dear,
> and his love made them strong;
> and they followed the right,

> for Jesus' sake,
> the whole of their good lives long.
> And one was a soldier,
>   and one was a priest,
> and one was slain by a fierce wild beast:
> and there's not any reason—
> no, not the least,
>   why I shouldn't be one too.
>
> They lived not only in ages past,
> there are hundreds of thousands still,
> the world is bright with the joyous saints
> who love to do Jesus' will.
> You can meet them in school, or in lanes,
>   or at sea,
> in church, or in trains, or in shops, or at tea,
> for the saints of God are just folk like me,
> and I mean to be one too
> (words: Lesbia Scott; music: "Grand Isle"
> by John Henry Hopkins, *The Hymnal
> 1982 According to the Use of the
> Episcopal Church* [New York: The
> Church Hymnal Corporation, 1985]).

This session is both an ice-breaker and a means of integrating our daily lives with our lives as saints-in-training.

Exercise

1. Give each participant white poster board. Everyone draws and cuts out a doll-sized outline of themselves. Create self-portraits by drawing clothing and features (hair, glasses, jewelry, etc.) that illustrate themselves. Add symbols of their ministry (lectionary for lectors, chalice for communion ministers, etc.) or spiritual life (rosary, Bible, etc.). On the backs, participants draw their favorite saint or religious inspiration (Mother Teresa, for example). If their art skills are minimal, a name and a symbol are sufficient ("St. Peter" and a set of keys, for example). Some participants may not have a favorite saint; keep a dictionary of saints handy for reference.

2. Invite each person to explain his or her self-portrait:

   • What role does his or her ministry or spiritual life play in his or her life as a saint-in-training?

   • How does his or her chosen saint or religious mentor inspire and encourage him or her as part of the communion of saints?

3. Tape each self-portrait on the walls all around the room, paper hand-in-hand.

Rite: All Saints

LEADER:
In the name of the Father, and of the Son, and of the Holy Spirit.

ALL:
Amen.

LEADER:
(*Read Eph 2:1-2,4-5,8-10,13,19-22.*)
Lord, have mercy.

ALL:
Lord, have mercy.

LEADER:
Christ, have mercy.

ALL:
Christ, have mercy.

LEADER:
Lord, have mercy.

ALL:
Lord, have mercy. (*As* LEADER *reads the "Litany of the Saints" (from* The Roman Missal*), respond after each saint: "Pray for us.")*

LEADER:
Holy Mary, Mother of God.
St. Michael.
Holy angels of God.
St. John the Baptist.
St. Joseph.
St. Peter and St. Paul.
St. Andrew.
St. John.
St. Mary Magdalene.
St. Stephen.
St. Ignatius.
St. Lawrence.
St. Perpetua and St. Felicity.
St. Agnes.
St. Gregory.
St. Augustine.
St. Athanasius.
St. Basil.
St. Martin.
St. Benedict.
St. Francis and St. Dominic.
St. Francis Xavier.
St. John Vianney.
St. Catherine.
St. Teresa.
(*Add participants' favorite saints if not in the litany.*)
All holy men and women.

Lord, be merciful.

ALL:
Lord, save your people.

LEADER:
From all evil.

ALL:
Lord, save your people.

LEADER:
From every sin.

ALL:
Lord, save your people.

LEADER:
From everlasting death.

ALL:
Lord, save your people.

LEADER:
By your incarnation.

ALL:
Lord, save your people.

LEADER:
By your resurrection.

ALL:

Lord, save your people.

LEADER:

By your gift of the Holy Spirit.

ALL:

Lord, save your people.

LEADER:

Be merciful to us sinners.

ALL:

Lord, hear our prayer. (*Sing "For all the Saints."*)

21. OUR LADY OF GUADALUPE

Season or Occasion

- Feast of Our Lady of Guadalupe, December 12
- Marian devotional occasions

Purpose

- to honor Our Lady of Guadalupe, Patroness of the Americas
- to experience another culture's vision of Mary (in this case, the Mexican-American) and to explore additional Marian themes and symbols

Symbol

The basic symbol for this session is the same created in session 2: an abbreviated rosary made of silk roses and vines with a crucifix at the end. Roses, always special to Mary, are especially significant in the story of Our Lady of Guadalupe. Added to this symbol is a picture of Our Lady of Guadalupe and a Mexican blanket to represent the *tilma* of Juan Diego.

Materials

- twenty red silk roses
- one length artificial vine
- one crucifix
- one picture of Our Lady of Guadalupe
- one Mexican blanket
- twist ties or florist's wire
- silk rose for each participant (optional)
- "scroll" printed with Prayer to Our Lady of Guadalupe for each participant (optional)

Introduction

In 1531, the Blessed Virgin appeared to the Indian Juan Diego at Tepeyac, a hill outside Mexico City. In response to the miraculous image of Mary that appeared on Juan Diego's *tilma* (worker's apron), Bishop Juan de Zumarraga built the first church there.

The complete story is told during the rite. It may be done entirely by one narrator, as a reader's theater piece by different participants, or as a pre-rehearsed mini-play with costumes and actions.

Exercises

1. If desired, participants may make their own "mini-rosaries" by using the strings of tiny satin-ribbon roses available in fabric and craft stores or by making knots in red and/or pink satin ribbon. After forming a circlet with the ribbon, attach a stick cross or image of Our Lady of Guadalupe.

Rite: Our Lady of Guadalupe

LEADER:
In the name of the Father, and of the Son, and of the Holy Spirit.

ALL:
Amen.

LEADER:
O Lady of Guadalupe, how kind you were to appear to the Indian convert Juan Diego, leaving your image on his *tilma*. In this way, you won many hearts for Christ. As devotion to you flourished over the centuries, you became patroness of Mexico and the Americas, and especially of the poor. Through your intercession, may more and more people accept your dear Son as their Lord.

ALL:
Amen.

READER 1:
(*Read Zech 2:10-13.*)

READER 2:
(*Read Lk 1:46-47,48-49,50-51,51-52,53, 54-55.*)

ALL:
(*Respond after each verse:*) God has done great things for me.
Holy is his name.

READER 3:
(*Read Rev 11:19; 12:1-6,10.*)

NARRATOR:
The story of Juan Diego and Our Lady of Guadalupe.

The Spanish conquest of Mexico was begun by Hernando Cortez in the year 1500. But despite the destruction of the pagan temples of human sacrifice, and despite the presence of Spanish Franciscan and Dominican priests, there were few Indian converts to Christianity. Then in the year 1531, something extraordinary happened.

Scene 1

On December 9, an Aztec Indian convert named Juan Diego was going to Mass. As he walked from his village to Mexico City a few miles south, he heard a woman's voice cry, "Juan Diego! Juanito!" Climbing a hill called Tepeyac, Juan saw a woman standing among the rocks. She was a beautiful young Indian girl dressed in a pink dress and a blue-green cloak. Although it was before sunrise, she was bathed in golden light.

"Dear son, I am the Mother of God. Hurry to the city and tell the bishop that I wish a church to be built on this hill."

Scene 2

Trembling with nervousness, Juan Diego went to see the bishop, Fray Juan de Zumarraga. The bishop was busy with important affairs, but he stopped to listen to Juan's story.

"Thank you for telling me of the vision, Juan Diego," said the bishop. "I believe you are sincere. But I'm afraid no one will attend a church built in the middle of nowhere! Let me think it over."

Returning to Tepeyac hill at sunset, the weary Juan Diego found the Mother of God waiting for him. "Forgive me, Lady. I've failed you! Please send someone else to convince the bishop."

The Lady answered, "My little son, I've chosen you to convince him to build my church. Return to the bishop tomorrow and ask him again."

Juan groaned inwardly but knelt before her. "Lady, I will obey you."

The next day, Juan Diego again asked the bishop to build a church for the Mother of God on Tepeyac hill.

"Yes, yes, Juan. I see you are in earnest! But I must have a sign from heaven before attempting to build this church," said the bishop firmly.

Juan Diego trudged back to the hill and told the Lady that the bishop asked for a sign.

"Very well," said the Lady. "Return at daybreak tomorrow and I'll give you a sign to convince the bishop."

Scene 3

However, when Juan Diego returned home that night, he found his elderly uncle desperately ill. Nursing his uncle that night and all the next day, Juan could not meet the Virgin Mary as planned.

"I'm going to die!" gasped his uncle. "Find a priest!"

As Juan ran down the rocky road, he met the Virgin Mary—although he had tried to avoid her because of his uncle's illness.

"Forgive me, Lady!" he panted. "My uncle is dying and I must find a priest. I can't talk about building your church right now."

The Lady said gently, "My dear son, I have cured your uncle. I will always protect and look after you. Now climb to the top of the hill and bring me the flowers growing there."

As he stumbled up the hill, Juan Diego moaned to himself in bewilderment, "How can my uncle be cured? How can I find roses growing among rocks in December? How will all this end?"

Yet when Juan reached the top of the hill, he found beautiful Castilian roses among the frost-covered cacti. Unfolding his coarse Aztec working apron (called a *tilma*), he filled it with roses and hurried back to the Virgin Mary. The Lady arranged them with her own hands. Then she tied the *tilma* around Juan's neck in such a way that the roses were concealed. Mary said, "Little son, take this sign to the bishop. This time he will believe you."

Scene 4

After hurrying to the bishop's house, Juan Diego excitedly told the story of his uncle's cure and Mary's arrangement of the roses. Then he untied the *tilma* from around his neck and the roses fell to the floor.

The bishop and several witnesses fell to their knees. For the *tilma* was imprinted with a beautiful image of the Virgin Mary.

"Castilian roses! A miraculous image of the Mother of God!" cried the bishop. "I shall build her church at once!" The bishop was so excited he insisted on seeing the hill right away.

While Juan Diego showed the bishop and his companions Tepeyac hill, Juan's uncle told them of his marvelous cure. Suddenly, the beautiful woman stood before them all, bathed in golden light. As they all fell to their knees, she said, "Call me Santa Maria de Guadalupe."

After the building of her church, throngs of native Indians converted to Catholicism

and she became the protective patroness
of Mexico.

LEADER:

Our Lady of Guadalupe,
     mystical rose,
intercede for the Holy Church,
protect the Holy Father,
help all who turn to you
     in their needs,
and, since you are ever
     the Virgin Mary
     and Mother of the true God,
obtain for us
     from your most holy Son,
the grace of keeping our faith,
sweet hope in the midst of the trials

of life,
burning charity,
and the precious gift
     of final perseverance
("Our Lady of Guadalupe Prayer"
Traditional Catholic Prayers).

ALL:
Amen.

(Conclude by singing an appropriate
Marian hymn. If you are in a part of the
country that traditionally celebrates the
Feast of Our Lady of Guadalupe, sing a
traditional song such as "Las Mananitas,"
"Quien Es Esa Estrella?" or "Adios, Oh
Virgen de Guadalupe.")

22. O ANTIPHONS

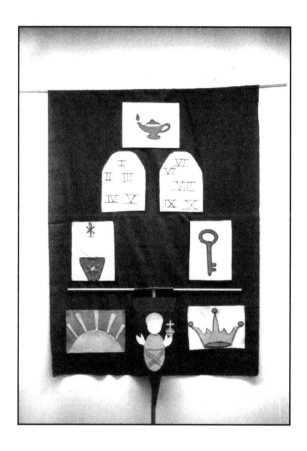

Season or Occasion

- Advent

Purpose

- to gain a deeper understanding of Advent through the "O Antiphons" (which we are most familiar with as the text of the song "O Come, O Come, Emmanuel") and other traditional texts

Symbol

This session uses the symbols traditionally associated with the "O Antiphons" (see chart on next page).

Materials

- felt (red, gold, blue, brown, flesh-colored, plus neutral colors)
- large length of solid heavy cloth
- black felt-tip pens
- long corsage pins
- banner pole
- pictures of crowns, keys, lamps, etc., from which the "craft-challenged" may copy symbol designs (optional)
- butcher paper for posting chart

Introduction

The "O Antiphons" are read during Evening Prayer of the Liturgy of the Hours from December 17 to December 23. They are familiar to us because we sing them during the four weeks of Advent as the song, "O Come, O Come, Emmanuel." The "O Antiphons" are full of the anticipation of the church as it awaits the coming of its Savior. Wisdom, Lord, Flower of Jesse, Key of David, Dayspring/Radiant Dawn, King of Nations, and Emmanuel are Old Testament images that the early church interpreted as foreshadowing Christ.

Christ is the Wisdom that governs creation and guided God's chosen people and all of salvation history. He is the Son of the Lord of ancient Israel, who liberated the chosen peo-

ple and gave them the law. Jesse was the father of David, who was anointed by the prophet to establish a royal family. Born of the royal line in Bethlehem, city of David, Christ is a sign for all peoples. The Key of David is a symbol of the promised redeemer who will liberate his people from sin and death. Christ is the Rising Sun, the Sun of Justice (Mal 3:19-20), the Light who shines on those who dwell in darkness. He is also King of all Nations, Gentile as well as Jew. Finally, the Christ child is Emmanuel, the "God with us" desire of nations.

For this session's rite, you may wish to assign the readings to participants rather than do them by yourself.

Exercises

TITLE	SCRIPTURE	SYMBOL
1. Emmanuel	Isa 7:14	Mother and Child
2. Wisdom	Dan 2:20	Lamp and flame
3. Lord of Might/ Leader of Israel	Deut 9:3	Ten Commandments
4. Flower/Root of Jesse's Stem	Isa 11:1-5 1 Sam 16:1-3	Blooming plant with Star of David and Chi-Rho
5. Key of David	Isa 22:22	Key
6. Dayspring/ Radiant Dawn	Isa 9:2	Rising Sun
7. Desire/King of Nations	Jer 10:7	Crown

1. Copy the information in the table above onto butcher paper and post where all can see it. (You may wish to write it out on a sheet of paper and photocopy for each participant). Discuss the titles of God in the

song "O Come, O Come, Emmanuel" and their corresponding Scripture references and symbols.

- What role does the Old Testament play in foretelling the coming of the Messiah?
- What role does hope play in our lives as Catholics during Advent? During our entire lives?
- What do these traditional titles and symbols of God mean in our personal faith-lives?

2. Create the symbols listed in the third column of the table by drawing, cutting out, or pasting them together.

3. Play a verse or two of "O Come, O Come, Emmanuel" and ask participants what feelings and memories this traditional tune rouses in them. This song comes from the ninth century.

- What role does the unbroken line of tradition play in Catholic faith?

Rite: O Antiphons

("*O Antiphon*" *texts taken from the Advent volume of* The Liturgy of the Hours).

(*A blank banner hangs at the front of the gathering space.*)

LEADER:
In the name of the Father, and of the Son, and of the Holy Spirit.

ALL:
Amen.

LEADER:
During this season of Advent, we gather to anticipate the coming of the Christ child—Emmanuel, which means "God with us."

READER 1:
(*Read Isa 11:1-10.*)

READER 2:
(*Read Ps 89:2-3,4-5,27,29.*)

ALL:
R. Forever I will sing the goodness of the Lord.

READER 3:
(*Read Lk 1:26-38.*)

(*During the following sequence, while the song "O Come, O Come Emmanuel" is sung, a participant processes forward carrying the symbol for that verse in one hand and a candle in the other. (If you have a large group, you may wish to have two people: one to hold the symbol and the other to hold the candle.) The symbol-candle bearers line up before the group so all can see clearly what they hold.*)

ALL:

O come, O come, Emmanuel,
and ransom captive Israel,
that mourns in lonely exile here
until the Son of God appear.

Rejoice! Rejoice! Emmanuel
shall come to you, O Israel.

LEADER:

Wisdom, O holy Word of God,
you govern all creation
with your strong yet tender care.
Come and show your people
the way to salvation.

ALL:

O come, thou Wisdom,
   from on high,
and order all things far and nigh;
to us the path of knowledge show,
and teach us in her ways to go.

Rejoice! Rejoice! Emmanuel
shall come to you, O Israel.

LEADER:

O sacred Lord of ancient Israel,
who showed yourself to Moses
in the burning bush,
who gave him the holy law
on Sinai mountain:
come, stretch out your mighty
hand to set us free.

ALL:

O come, O come,
   thou Lord of might,
who to thy tribes on Sinai's height
in ancient times did give the law
in cloud, and majesty, and awe.

Rejoice! Rejoice! Emmanuel
shall come to you, O Israel.

LEADER:

O Flower of Jesse's stem,
you have been raised up as a sign
for all peoples;
kings stand silent in your presence;
the nations bow down in worship
    before you.
Come, let nothing keep you
from coming to our aid.

ALL:

O come, thou Rod of Jesse's stem,
from ev'ry foe deliver them
that trust thy mighty power to save,
and give them vict'ry o'er the grave.

Rejoice! Rejoice! Emmanuel
shall come to you, O Israel.

LEADER:

O Key of David, O royal power
    of Israel
controlling at your will the gate
    of heaven:
come, break down the prison walls
    of death for those who dwell
    in darkness and the shadow
    of death;
and lead your captive people
    to freedom.

ALL:

O come, thou key of David, come,
and open wide our heav'nly home;
make safe the way that leads
    on high,
that we no more have cause
    to sigh.

Rejoice! Rejoice! Emmanuel
shall come to you, O Israel.

LEADER:

O Radiant Dawn,
    splendor of eternal light,
sun of justice;
come shine on those who dwell
in darkness and the shadow
    of death.

ALL:

O come, thou Dayspring from
    on high,
and cheer us by thy drawing nigh;
disperse the gloomy clouds of night
and death's dark shadow put
    to flight.

Rejoice! Rejoice! Emmanuel
shall come to you, O Israel.

LEADER:

O King of all the nations,
    the only joy
    of every human heart;
O Keystone of the mighty arch
    of man,
come and save the creature
    you fashioned from the dust.

ALL:

O come, Desire of nations, bind
in one the hearts of all mankind;
bid every strife and quarrel cease
and fill the world
    with heaven's peace.

Rejoice! Rejoice! Emmanuel
shall come to you, O Israel.

LEADER:

O Emmanuel, king and lawgiver,
desire of the nations,
Savior of all people,
come and set us free,
Lord of God.

ALL:

O come, O come, Emmanuel,
and ransom captive Israel
that mourns in lonely exile here
until the Son of God appear.

Rejoice! Rejoice! Emmanuel
shall come to you, O Israel.

LEADER:
Lord, show us your mercy and love.

ALL:
And grant us your salvation.

LEADER:
Come and set us free, Lord God of power
and might.

ALL:
Let your face shine upon us and we shall
be saved.

LEADER:
Come, Lord, do not delay.

ALL:
Free your people from sinfulness.

LEADER:
God of love and mercy, help us to follow
the example of Mary, always ready to do
your will. At the message of an angel, she
welcomed your eternal Son and, filled
with the light of your Spirit, she became
the temple of your Word, who lives and
reigns with you and the Holy Spirit, one
God, for ever and ever.

In the name of the Father, and of the Son,
and of the Holy Spirit.

ALL:
Amen.

*(When the rite has concluded, pin each
symbol to the banner for display and line
up the candles underneath on a table.)*

23. CHRISTMAS STATIONS

Season or Occasion

- Advent
- Christmas

Purpose

- to experience the progression of Christmas texts by means of mini "Christmas stations" based on the Mexican "Las Posadas" festival

Symbol

A set of "Christmas stations" to match the text of this session's rite are placed at intervals around a large, empty space.

Materials

- felt or construction paper to make stations
- a banner pole (I made mine from an old kitchen mop)
- glue
- brown paper lunch bags
- candles
- scissors
- black felt-tip pens

Introduction

On Christmas Eve a candlelight
to shine abroad through Christmas night,
That those who pass may see its glow,
and walk with Christ a mile or so
(Wernecke 50).

This simple verse refers to the old Irish custom of placing a candle in the window to guide Mary and Joseph on their journey to Bethlehem and to invite wanderers in for a meal and lodging. Dating from the infamous Penal Times when Catholicism and the Mass were treason, it also served to alert Catholics to the presence of an illegal priest.

The Christmas event in Scripture is a time of uncertain journeys, strangers in a strange land, and reliance on God's glorious promises. This session allows participants to "walk with Christ a mile or so" as they explore the uncertainties and expectations of the season. It is loosely based on the Hispanic tradition of "Las Posadas" (*posada* means "inn"). From December 16 to Christmas Eve, nine nightly processions help to re-enact the struggle of Mary and Joseph to safely reach Bethlehem and find lodging. Dating back to St. Ignatius Loyola—who suggested that nine days of special prayers be said—it was St. John of the Cross who created the actual religious pageant in 1580. Spanish missionaries carried it to Mexico, where it was celebrated in private homes within the community.

Exercises

1. Everyone has taken a trip to a strange place that did not go as planned; many have been stranded temporarily by mechanical failures in a car or airplane.

   - How does you feel when you are powerless to change your situation?
   - How did you handle these feelings?
   - As earthly pilgrims journeying toward heaven, how do you feel when unforeseen hitches delay or detour that journey?
   - Do you try to rely on God or yourself when problems occur?
   - How can we strengthen our trust in God as the great Navigator of our journey?

2. Make the Christmas stations and luminaries as part of the session. You may wish to have pictures of each symbol from which participants may get ideas for drawing. The stations consist of:

   - a candle
   - an angel
   - Joseph leading Mary on a donkey
   - a sheep with shepherd's crook and a star
   - the star over the empty manger

Under each station is placed a "luminaria" (a brown paper bag with a candle inside); each luminaria has a star cut out from the front. Participants carry candles or lanterns as they progress from station to station. The procession is led by a banner with the image of a star.

Rite: Christmas Stations

(Angel banner leads procession from station to station and stops at each banner, marked by luminaria, while the appropriate reading is read and song is sung. Then the procession moves to the next station. Stations can be hung on the wall, held by participants, hung from banners, the ceiling.)

LEADER
(Begin with an appropriate opening prayer.)

STATION/READING 1:
Isaiah 9:2,6-7

STATION/READING 2:
Isaiah 7:14

ALL:
(Sing verse 1 of "O Come, O Come, Emmanuel" while moving to the next station.)

STATION/READING 3:
Luke 1:26-38

ALL:
(Sing verses 1 and 2 of "Of the Father's Love Begotten" while moving to the next station.)

STATION/READING 4:
Luke 2:1-7

ALL:
(Sing verse 1 of "O Little Town of Bethlehem" while moving to the next station.)

STATION/READING 5:
Luke 2:8-12

ALL:
(Sing verses 1 and 2 of "Silent Night" while moving to the next station.)

STATION/READING 6:
Luke 2:13-16

ALL:
(Sing verse 1 of "Angels We Have Heard on High.")

24. LITTLE JUGGLER PLAY

Season or Occasion

- Christmas
- any Marian occasion
- ministry retreat

Purpose

- to creatively explore the spiritual meaning of individual gifts and how they integrate with ministry

Symbol

For this session's symbol you may adapt the symbol of Mary and Jesus from session 1. During the playlet, the symbolic gifts of each participant will be laid before Our Lady. The character of the juggler offers golden juggling balls (felt attached to the image of Mary.). If prior preparation is possible, call participants and ask them to bring symbols of their gift or vocation. Parents may present their children's toys, medical personnel a stethoscope, business people a calculator, gardeners a plant, communion ministers a bottle of wine, lectors the Bible, etc. If prior preparation is not possible, have each person draw a symbol of their gift on paper for presentation to the group.

Materials

- an image of the Virgin Mary (from session 1 if desired)
- costumes for the playlet (if none are available, hang name tags with the character's name around each actor's neck)

Introduction

This session is based on the story of the little juggler of Notre Dame. A tale that has been told a hundred times, it bears retelling because each generation must learn to discern the false prophets of its time.

Exercises

1. Read 1 Corinthians 12:4-31; 13:1-13.

   - What is each participant's experience of the pooling of many talents and resources?
   - How have their lives been enriched by this?

2. Read 1 Corinthians 1:18-26.

   - How is secular wisdom inappropriate to the pilgrim church?
   - How have we been "fools for Christ," daring the ridicule of others as the little juggler did?
   - If we haven't had the courage, how can we take that daring first step?

Rite: Little Juggler Play

(The scene is set inside a medieval cathedral. Townspeople mill about excitedly as they wait for an important religious procession to begin. They ad-lib comments such as: "I'm so excited! I can't wait to see the procession!" "We travel in from the country every year for the feast." "Do you like my new dress for the festival?" JUGGLER plies his trade on the edge of the crowd, but even he is distracted. GUARD enters and shouts orders at the crowd, waving his spear.)

GUARD:
Make way! Make way for Master Mercado the Merchant! You riffraff quit blocking his view of the procession!

ONLOOKER 1:
If he wants to see the procession so bad, why doesn't he buy one of his own?

ONLOOKER 2:
He already did! He bought that fancy new image of the Blessed Virgin just so people will think he's important.

ONLOOKER 1:
I'm surprised Master Mercado didn't throw in a new cathedral while he was at it.

ONLOOKER 2:
He would have if somebody hadn't beaten him to it a hundred years ago.

GUARD:
Make way! Make way!

(Enter MASTER MERCADO THE MERCHANT, very haughty and finely dressed in medieval clothes with flashy colors and lots of gold jewelry. He sails past the crowd, holding a handkerchief to his nose to block their smell. The JUGGLER is so awed by the fine gentleman that he

drops his juggling balls. They roll under Mercado's feet and he stumbles, almost falling flat.)*

JUGGLER:
(Greatly distressed) Forgive me, Master Mercado! I didn't mean to hurt you! I'm not a very good juggler yet. *(GUARD shoves him away and assists his master, who ignores the street-player, straightens his clothes, and regains his dignity with difficulty. The crowd cries out.)*

ALL:
The procession is coming!
The procession is coming!

(Singing a Marian hymn, the procession enters, carrying an image of the Mother and Child. At this point, the Baby's hands are empty. All onlookers reverently remove their hats and makes signs of the cross.)

GUARD:
Behold this fine new image of Our Lady that Master Mercado has so graciously donated!

(ALL applaud, some sarcastically, some without enthusiasm. MERCADO struts proudly up to the image, admires it, pretends to dust off the surface, and frowns at imaginary flaws. He shows no reverence to the Mother and Child at all. He bows to the applauding crowd with mock modesty. Enter the cathedral RECTOR. He is pleased with the image but not so pleased that Mercado donated it. MERCADO kneels with exaggerated piety for the Rector's blessing. The crowd kneels too.)

RECTOR:
Our thanks to Master Mercado for this beautiful image of the Blessed Mother and

her Child. May heaven reward you as you deserve.

JUGGLER:
(*Tosses his hat into the air*) Hip-hip hooray!

MERCADO:
(*Frowns*) Be quiet, boy! How dare you be so disrespectful of the church?

JUGGLER:
(*Repentant*) I wasn't being disrespectful, Master Mercado. Our Lady is so lovely, I couldn't help cheering. (*Draws closer to the image*) But the baby has nothing to play with. (*Turns to MERCADO*) Is the Baby Jesus as poor as I am?

MERCADO:
(*Pushes him aside*) The Baby Jesus, poor like you? What an insult! Go cheer in some place suitable for a gutter boy, like a pigsty or a tavern! (*Resumes his overly respectful, solemn manner.*) Reverend Father, please allow me to make another humble donation to our glorious cathedral. (*Snaps his fingers and GUARD brings forward an object wrapped in fine cloth. MERCADO unwraps a fabulous-looking chalice. He reverently lays the chalice before the Mother and Child.*) A poor offering, but the best I can give the Queen of Heaven and her Son.

RECTOR:
(*Politely, but unenthusiastically*) Thank you, my son.

(*The townspeople file forward and lay their gifts before the image. JUGGLER juggles wildly out of sheer excitement on the fringe of the crowd.*)

MERCADO:
(*Drawing RECTOR aside, confidentially*) Reverend Father, I wanted to ask you a question. Have you considered my request to be buried inside the cathedral?

Just a simple little tombstone before the high altar. You'll hardly notice it. (*RECTOR rolls his eyes as if begging heaven for patience. MERCADO continues to press his suit in a hurried undertone. The crowd finishes its offerings and only the little JUGGLER is left.*)

GUARD:
Hurry up, boy! Make your offering! Don't keep us waiting!

JUGGLER:
(*Sadly*) I'm only a poor juggler. I have nothing to give Our Lady and the Baby Jesus. Nothing wonderful like Master Mercado gave. (*Looks closely at the image.*) But Baby Jesus has no toys to play with. How sad! All these gifts are too heavy and grown-up for him.

MERCADO:
(*Irritated*) What's this interruption? Oh, it's you again! Go away. Our Lady wants to see her wonderful gifts, not a dirty street boy. Shoo! Shoo!

(*The crowd mutters. Some agree with Mercado;, some sympathize with the Juggler. JUGGLER starts to leave.*)

RECTOR:
Wait, my son. Here's something to give the Blessed Mother. (*Removes his gold cross and places it in the Juggler's hands.*) She'll understand it's from both of us.

JUGGLER:
(*Bows to the image*) Here, my Lady, this is for you and your Son. (*Lays the cross before the image. The crowd approves; MERCADO is insulted.*) But I still wish I had something of my own to give.

RECTOR:
Someday you will, my son.

MERCADO:
(*Shoving his way forward, shoving JUGGLER aside*) Come, my dear Rector. It's time for the feast!

CROWD:
The feast! It's time for the feast! Hooray!

MERCADO:
(*Leading RECTOR away*) I've ordered all your favorite foods, Reverend Father. The finest wines! The sweetest pastries! And I got a wonderful deal on the best venison you ever tasted. It will melt in your mouth.

(*ALL exit excitedly, except JUGGLER, hat in hand, looking wistfully at the Mother and Child.*)

JUGGLER:
I still wish there was something of my own I could give you, my Lady.

VOICE OFFSTAGE:
Come on, juggler boy! They want you to perform for the feast!

(*JUGGLER puts on his hat, gathers his equipment and scampers offstage.*)

(*The feast is over; night has fallen and the passage of time is indicated by townspeople crossing the stage, yawning and ad-libbing complimentary remarks about the feast. JUGGLER creeps back into the church with a candle. Looking cautiously around, he sets the candle down at the feet of the image of the Mother and Child. He bows before the image, holds out his juggling balls and solemnly addresses the image.*)

JUGGLER:
This is my only gift, but I dedicate it to you both, my Mother and my Savior. (*He juggles, grows sleepy, juggles more slowly. He drops a ball and it rolls away from sight.*) Oh bother! I'll look for it in the morning. I'm too sleepy right now. (*Yawns and curls up at the foot of the image.*)

(*Morning comes. MASTER MERCADO slips stealthily into the cathedral. He doesn't see the Juggler asleep in a corner but goes straight to the gifts piled under the image and picks up his chalice. He is about to hide it under his clothes when RECTOR enters. He catches MERCADO, who straightens up and looks guilty. RECTOR stops short and looks surprised.*)

MERCADO:
(*Heartily*) Good morning, Rector! No ill-effects from last night's feast, I trust? (*Pretends to polish the chalice.*)

RECTOR:
At your prayers so early, my son?

MERCADO:
Just came to see that the image and gifts came to no harm. You never know what riffraff might get into the cathedral. Hey! Hey! Juggler boy! Wake up! (*Shakes JUGGLER awake.*)

JUGGLER:
I'm sorry, sir. I must have fallen asleep. I wasn't doing anything wrong.

MERCADO:
What are you doing here? Come to steal something? (*Hastily checks the pile of gifts.*)

JUGGLER:
I gave my gift to Our Lady last night. I juggled for her and the Baby.

MERCADO:
Sacrilege! Desecration! Rector, throw this street scum out!

RECTOR:
(*Calmly*) The little juggler gave the best he had. Just as you did, Master Mercado. (*Looks pointedly at the chalice, which*

MERCADO *gives a hasty rub and puts back on the gift pile.)*

JUGGLER:
One of the balls I juggle with is missing! What will I do? I can't perform without it! *(They hunt for the ball. They find it in the hand of the Baby Jesus, or placed closely by him.)* Why, there it is! The Baby Jesus has it!

RECTOR:
(Picks up ball, almost drops it) This ball has become very heavy!

MERCADO:
And it's changed color. It looks like...gold! *(Snatches the ball from RECTOR.)* The ball has turned to solid gold!

JUGGLER:
Oh good! The Baby Jesus turned it into a nicer present. It was all dirty before.

MERCADO:
(Strokes the ball lovingly) I'll see you get another ball to juggle with, my boy.

RECTOR:
(Takes the ball and places it back with the image) Indeed you will, Master Mercado. Why don't you go to the marketplace and buy one now while I proclaim this miracle to the entire town?

MERCADO:
Why, yes, Reverend Father! Of course, Reverend Father! Whatever you wish. *(Turns to JUGGLER respectfully)* And whatever *you* wish too, my little man! Can I buy you some breakfast? A new suit of clothes? Do you think this gift of turning objects into gold might work for a poor, hardworking merchant like myself?

RECTOR:
Making this lad the star performer at the feast celebrating this miracle seems appropriate.

MERCADO:
A feast! Another feast! With an exhibition of juggling! What a wonderful idea! At once, Reverend Father! *(Heads for the door.)* Guard! Guard! Come quickly! Get my caterer. Get my tailor. We're throwing another party in thanksgiving for this glorious miracle! *(Exits.)*

RECTOR:
Lad, while Merchant Mercado prepares to give thanks, let us give thanks as well. As you can see, no gift is too small to offer the Blessed Mother and the Baby Jesus. *(RECTOR and JUGGLER kneel at the foot of the image.)*

25. HOLY INNOCENTS

Season or Occasion

- Feast of the Holy Innocents, December 28
- a pro-life exercise
- a ceremony of healing for those grieving for lost children

Purpose

- to help heal grief for innocent children abused by society
- to unite in support of pro-life

Symbol

The symbol is a "newborn" baby doll (available in large toy stores). Dressed only in a diaper and laid in a simple, homemade crib, it shows the utter helplessness and dependency of all babies.

Materials

- a life-size baby doll to represent "lost children"
- a layette set for the doll (diaper, baby clothes, receiving blanket, toys), ideally created by the participants
- small crib or manger to lay the doll in
- holy water

Introduction

The Feast of the Holy Innocents dates from the year 505. It is one of the saints' feasts following Christmas which people in the Middle Ages called the "Companions of Christ" ("Comites Christi"). These saints—Stephen, the apostle John, the Holy Innocents—were regarded as honor guards accompanying the Christ child. Medieval commentators described them as models of three forms of martyrdom: voluntary and executed (Stephen), voluntary but not executed (John), executed but not voluntary (Holy Innocents).

Gordon Lathrop writes:

> Just as it is the crucified who is "Messiah"
> so it is the crucified who is Sun and
> Light-Tree and the end of darkness and
> the world's health....It is further evident in
> the themes of the littleness and
> hiddenness and humility of the birth,
> present in hymnody and readings,
> themselves sub-themes of the Cross, or
> in the Cross references of the readings
> ("A sword will pierce through your own
> soul also"), or, most especially in the
> feasts which have very anciently
> accompanied the day of Christmas (the
> feasts of the "Comites Christi," which
> Durandus called them in the 13th
> century as the "companions of Christ").
> This Sun is hated by the rulers of the
> world and his Cross is foreshadowed in
> the sufferings of the Innocents and in all
> unjust sufferings....It is "only in these our
> Christian mysteries that we can rejoice
> and mourn at once for the same reason"
> (T. S. Eliot in *Murder in the Cathedral*)
> (*A Christmas Sourcebook* 70).

While the secular world ignores the foreshadowing of the cross that the Christmas season carries, preferring the superficial frivolity of commercialism, Catholics can draw strength by exploring this "shadow side." This session first honors the memory of the Holy Innocents murdered by Herod in his attempt to find the Christ child. Second, it is an opportunity to unite in support of the pro-life struggle, which has never ceased to be fought since King Herod's time. Third, this exercise is a chance to seek healing for the loss of children through abortion, miscarriage, violence, neglect, kidnapping, accident, or other untimely death.

Many traditional Catholic devotions to the Christ child exist in different cultures. As modern secularism has devalued children, who were once considered so precious (children were vital to ancient Judaic culture, for example), these devotions have fallen into disuse. However, this session uses the theme of the Holy Child and his Mother to tap into the "shadow grief" that many adults carry concerning lost children and to promote the healing process. Since this session has many applications, it may be used year-round, not merely on December 28. It is interesting that the Feast of the Holy Family is celebrated within the Octave of Christmas. It juxtaposes the martyrs' feasts of this period with the classic Catholic symbol of warmth, nurturing and protection: the Holy Family.

Exercises

1. Part of this session's rite consists of symbolically "caring" for lost children, represented by a doll. As preparation for the rite, participants may wish to make their own layette set for the child.

2. If this prayer service is used for pro-life purposes rather than to grieve for a specific child, read Jeremiah 1:5 and discuss the following:

- How does this passage express the Catholic stance on the value of life?
- What implications does it have in the "real world" and how do we bear witness to that world?

- What steps can I take to spiritually adopt a baby? (Many diocesan Human Life Offices provide materials that explain, step-by-step, what level of development a spiritually adopted baby reaches over nine months.)
- What spiritual benefits does this exercise provide for myself and others?

Rite: Holy Innocents

LEADER:
In the name of the Father, and of the Son, and of the Holy Spirit.

ALL:
Amen.

LEADER:
We have gathered here to honor the memory of all Holy Innocents—the children lost to us through abortion, war, violence, neglect, accident, abduction, and untimely death. In reparation to the lost children of the world, let us listen to the Word of God.

READER 1:
(Read Jer 31:15-17.)

READER 2:
(Read Jer 1:5.)

ALL:
Before I formed you in the womb I knew you, before you were born, I dedicated you.

READER 2:
(Read Mt 2:13-18.)

ALL:
Before I formed you in the womb I knew you, before you were born, I dedicated you.

READER 3:
(Read Mt 18:1-5; 19:13-15.)

LEADER:
As a wreath laid on the Tomb of the Unknown Soldier symbolically honors all the war dead, so this prayer service will honor all Holy Innocents, named or nameless. (At this point, the doll, dressed in a diaper, is brought forward ceremoniously and carefully held in the hands of one participant.) This is the symbol of our Holy Innocents, the lost children of the world. To begin the process of reclaiming these lost children, we will now "name" the child. Please pass the child gently from one person to the next. As you hold the baby, think of a lost child you know, and give the baby that name. Or name the baby in honor of the millions of children who never lived to be named by their parents. You may speak the name aloud or remain silent. (The doll is passed from person to person. Each participant meditates on the name bestowed on the baby before passing it on to the next person, until finally it reaches LEADER.) God of glory, whom we name in many ways, we bring this child to your church.

READER 1:
What name do you give this child?

LEADER:
Let us all meditate on the name we have bestowed on this child in our hearts. (Silence) We name this child as a member of the Holy Family. It has come safely to that place where its name is written in the Book of Life.

ALL:
Amen.

LEADER:
With great joy, we welcome this child as a member of the Christian community. In its name, we claim you for your brother Christ, the infant Jesus, by the signs of water and the cross. With holy water, I now trace the cross on this baby's forehead. I invite all here present to do the same.

(LEADER *uses holy water to make the sign of the cross on the baby. One by one, all present come forward and do the same. During this process, ALL recite the Litany of the Infant Jesus (adapted from "Litany of the Infant Jesus,"* New Saint Joseph Prayer Book [*New York, Catholic Book Publishing Co., 1980*].

ALL:

Lord have mercy.
Christ have mercy.
Lord, have mercy.
Jesus, hear us.
Jesus, graciously hear us.
God the Father of heaven,
    have mercy on us.
God the Son, Redeemer
    of the world,
    have mercy on us.
God, the Holy Spirit,
    have mercy on us.
Holy Trinity, one God,
    have mercy on us.
Infant Jesus Christ,
    have mercy on us.
Infant, true God, have mercy on us.
Infant, Son of the living God,
    have mercy on us.
Infant, Son of the Virgin Mary,
    have mercy on us.
Infant, strong in weakness,
    have mercy on us.
Infant, powerful in tenderness,
    have mercy on us.
Infant, treasure in grace,
    have mercy on us.
Infant, fountain of love,
    have mercy on us.
Infant, renewer of the heavens,
    have mercy on us.
Infant, repairer of the evils of earth,
    have mercy on us.

Infant, head of the angels,
    have mercy on us.
Infant, root of the patriarchs,
    have mercy on us.
Infant, speech of the prophets,
    have mercy on us.
Infant, desire of the Gentiles,
    have mercy on us.
Infant, joy of shepherds,
    have mercy on us.
Infant, light of the Magi,
    have mercy on us.
Infant, salvation of infants,
    have mercy on us.
Infant, expectation of the just,
    have mercy on us.
Infant, instructor of the wise,
    have mercy on us.
Infant, first fruits of all saints,
    have mercy on us.

LEADER:
We have named this child. We have claimed it as a member of the Holy Family and placed it in the care of its brother, Jesus. As a sign that we cherish this child and all children, we will now clothe and lay it securely to rest.

(*While selected participants come forward to clothe the child with clothes and blanket and lay it in the cradle or manger, ALL recite the rest of the Litany of the Infant Jesus.*)

ALL:

Be merciful, spare us, O Infant
Jesus.
Be merciful, graciously hear us,
    O Infant Jesus.
From the slavery of the children
    of Adam, Infant Jesus, deliver us.

(*The following intercessions are adapted from "Order for the Blessing of Children"* Book of Blessings.)

LEADER:

The Lord Jesus held up to all his followers the simplicity and trust of children as a condition for entering the kingdom of heaven. Let us therefore call on Jesus in prayer, saying:

ALL:

Lord, in children let us welcome you.

LEADER:

Lord Jesus, born of the Virgin Mary, you sanctified childhood; grant that all children may have the chance to grow as you did in wisdom, age, and grace.

ALL:

Lord, in children let us welcome you.

LEADER:

Let us as caregivers and as a church show all children the tenderness of your own love; grant that those entrusted with the care of children be tireless in watching over them.

ALL:

Lord, in children let us welcome you.

LEADER:

Even as a child you had to undergo persecution and exile; grant that all children who are victims of the evil of these times may find help and protection.

ALL:

Lord, in children let us welcome you.

LEADER:

Many cultures are devoted to your childhood under many names, such as Holy Child of Atocha and the Infant of Prague. May our reverence to your childhood give us reverence for the innocence and vulnerability of all children.

ALL:

Lord, in children let us welcome you.

(LEADER *invites spontaneous intercessions. The Litany is then concluded.*)

Through your pure conception,
through your humble Nativity,
through your glorious Epiphany,
through your presentation in the
Temple,
through your life in poverty,
ministry,
    suffering and love,
Lamb of God, you take away the
sins
    of the world,
Have mercy on us, O Infant Jesus.
Lamb of God, you take away the
sins
    of the world,
Graciously hear us, O Infant Jesus.
Lamb of God, you take away the
sins
    of the world,
Grant us peace.

LEADER:

Jesus, friend of children, bless the children of the whole world.

Let us praise and thank the Lord, who took the little children into his arms to protect them from anger, indifference and neglect. Praised be the Lord now and forever.

ALL:

Praised be the Lord now and forever.

LEADER:

In the name of the Father, and of the Son, and of the Holy Spirit.

ALL:

Amen. (*Sing or play a recording of the traditional carol, "Lullaby Thou Little Tiny Child," which tells the story of Herod and the Holy Innocents.*)

CITED AND SUGGESTED RESOURCES

Book of Blessings. Collegeville: The Liturgical Press, 1989.

A Book of Prayers. Washington, DC: International Commission on English in the Liturgy, 1982.

Catholic Household Blessings and Prayers. Washington, DC: United States Catholic Conference, 1988.

Catechism of the Catholic Church. Washington, DC: United States Catholic Conference, Inc.—Libreria Editrice Vaticana, 1994.

Collopy, George. *Extraordinary Banners for Ordinary Times*. San Jose: Resource Publications, Inc., 1992.

———. *It's a Banner Year! New Directions in No-Word Banners*. San Jose: Resource Publications, Inc., 1990.

Deiss, Lucien, ed. *Springtime of the Liturgy*. Chicago: Liturgy Training Publications, 1979.

An Easter Sourcebook: The Fifty Days. Edited by Gabe Huck Gabe, Gail Ramshaw, and Gordon Lathrop. Chicago: Liturgy Training Publications, Inc., 1988.

Evans, Francis, ed. *New Saint Joseph People's Prayer Book*. New York: Catholic Book Publishing Co., 1993.

Feister, John Bookser. "Free to Forgive." *St. Anthony Messenger* (Dec. 1992).

Guelzow, Diane. *Banners with Pizazz: A Step-by-Step Guide*. San Jose: Resource Publications, Inc., 1992.

Gurak, Eileen. *Using Art in Sunday Worship*. San Jose: Resource Publications, Inc., 1990.

Hynes, Mary Ellen. *Companion to the Calendar*. Chicago: Liturgy Training Publications, Inc., 1993.

Knuth, Jill. *Banners without Words*. San Jose: Resource Publications, Inc., 1986.

Krier, Catherine H. *Symbols for All Seasons: Environmental Planning for Cycles A, B, and C*. San Jose: Resource Publications, Inc., 1988.

Lectionary for Mass. Washington, DC: International Committee on English in the Liturgy, 1969.

A Lent Sourcebook: The Forty Days. 2 vols. Edited by Robert J. Baker, Evelyn Kaehler, and Peter Mazar. Chicago: Liturgy Training Publications, 1990.

The Liturgy of the Hours According to the Roman Rite. 4 vols. New York: Catholic Book Publishing Co., 1975.

Mazar, Peter. *To Crown the Year: Decorating the Church throughout the Seasons*. Chicago: Liturgy Training Publications, Inc., 1995.

Mischke, Bernard, OSC, and Fritz Mischke, OSC, editors. *Pray Today's Gospel*. New York: Alba House, 1980.

New St. Joseph Weekday Missal. 2 vols. New York: Catholic Book Publishing Co., 1975.

Noffke, Suzanne, OP, trans. *The Dialogue*. New York: Paulist, 1980.

Nugent, Frances Edward. *Fairest Star of All: A Little Treasury of Mariology*. Paterson, New Jersey: St. Anthony Guild Press, 1956.

Order of Christian Funerals. Chicago: Liturgy Training Publications, 1989.

Pennington, M. Basil, OSCO, and Dr. Yael Katzir. *Bernard of Clairvaux: A Saint's Life in Word and Image*. Huntington, Indiana: Our Sunday Visitor, 1994.

Post, W. Ellwood. *Saints, Signs and Symbols*. Wilton, Connecticut: Morehouse Publishing, 1974.

Rite of Christian Initiation of Adults. Chicago: Liturgy Training Publications, Inc., 1988.

The Rites of the Catholic Church. 3 vols. New York: Pueblo, 1976.

Simcoe, Mary Ann, ed. A Christmas Sourcebook. Chicago: Liturgy Training Publications, 1984.

Traditional Catholic Prayers. Edited by Msgr. Charles J. Dollen. Huntington, Indiana: Our Sunday Visitor, 1990.

A Triduum Sourcebook. Edited by Gabe Huck and Mary Ann Simcoe. Chicago: Liturgy Training Publications, Inc., 1983.

Walsh, Michael, ed. *Butler's Lives of the Saints*. Rev. ed. San Francisco: HarperSanFrancisco, 1991.

Wernecke, Herbert H. *Christmas Customs around the World*. Louisville, Kentucky: Westminster Press, 1959.

SYMBOLS FOR ALL SEASONS
Planning Worship Environments for Cycles A, B, and C

Catherine H. Krier

Paper, 175 pages

5" x 8", 0-89390-125-3

Chock-full of environment ideas and descriptions of symbols based on the Sunday lectionary readings of all three cycles, this book also gives you tips on liturgy planning, artistic considerations, and color.

USING ART IN SUNDAY WORSHIP

Eileen Gurak

Paper, 80 pages

5" x 8", 0-89390-186-5

The author distinguishes between religious and liturgical art and shows how to decorate and organize your worship space for maximum participation. Illustrated.

EXTRAORDINARY BANNERS
for Ordinary Times

George Collopy

Paper, 240 pages

6" x 9", 0-89390-225-X

Here are more than 100 exciting patterns that focus on ordinary times from an anniversary to an opening day. The classic patterns in this new book derive from two main sources: renaissance art and early American quilts.

IT'S A BANNER YEAR!

George Collopy

Paper, 136 pages

6" x 9", 0-89390-176-8

If you're looking for more banner ideas, you'll love these patterns from the award-winning art director of Modern Liturgy magazine. More than 100 banner and temporary-art designs for liturgical seasons, sacraments, and secular holidays. Designs have grid overlays for easy reproduction.

BANNERS WITH PIZAZZ
A Step-by-Step Guide

Diane Guelzow

Paper, Color Illustrations, 120 pages

6" x 9", 0-89390-208-X

This is not another pattern book. Learn about color, materials, and techniques that take you well beyond rectangles on felt. Step-by-step instructions for basic banner construction - and plenty of options will help you design your own banners! Filled with visual aids, including 12 color illustrations.

BANNERS WITHOUT WORDS

Jill Knuth

Paper, 198 pages

6" x 9", 0-89390-075-3

This collection of design ideas, illustrations, instructions, and handy tips will help you make your own beautiful, wordless banners. More than 50 reproducible designs!

CLIP ART
for Communicating the Good News

Jean Morningstar

Paper, 128 perforated pages

8" x 11", 0-89390-160-1

These drawings, a remarkable blend of simplicity and inspiration, illustrate passages from throughout the Bible, and cover the seasons of Advent, Christmas, Lent, Easter, and many other feasts. You can photocopy and use each full page as is or clip the graphics for use in your own designs. Great for Sunday bulletins, flyers, newsletters, student handouts, and stationery.

CLIP ART FOR CATECHESIS

George Collopy

200 images, TIFF file format

One IBM-PC compatible CD-ROM

Use this computer clip art for bulletins, banners, or lesson handouts. This catechetical set includes images for Advent, Christmas, Easter, Pentecost, and more. George Collopy, MODERN LITURGY's art director, created these popular sets which contain a variety of styles from modern to classic. Great for use with Microsoft Word, MS Works, WordPerfect, Ami Pro, or any desktop publishing software. The CD-ROM includes free demos for Liturgy Plus and Sacramental Register.

CLIP ART
for Bulletins and Beyond

George Collopy

Paper, 80 perforated pages

8" x 11", 0-89390-124-58

MS-DOS 3.5" HD diskettes,

224 images, 0-89390-337-X

Produce bulletins, banners, and programs with art appropriate for any Sunday of the liturgical year and in various sizes for your convenience. Learn how to make different bulletins using different folds, and how to enlarge art spots to your specifications. Available as a 125 page book or on diskette. With the diskette version, let your own computer graphic software change the size of each image, crop it, or even change its shape. Images are stored as TIFF files on the diskettes.

RCIA SPIRITUALITY
Formation for the Catechumenate Team

Barbara Hixon with Reflection Questions by Gael Gensler, OSF

Paper, 192 pages

5" x 8", 0-89390-399-X

Like the RCIA itself, this book is dangerous, scary, risky, an invitation to mayhem and mystery. Dont read it if you want to keep adult initiation and conversion something you do to others and not what God does to you. Rev. James B. Dunning, Barbara Hixon and Gael Gensler have a straightforward message: the catechumenal process is not something you do to someone else. It's something that happens to you, the team member, as much as to the catechumen. They take you deep into the spirituality of the catechumenate process and show you how each step from pre-catechumenate to mystagogia will change your life. Gail Gensler's questions help turn this book, a revision of the original RCIA Ministry, into a useful group formation tool for the catechumenate team.

TRANSFIGURATION CATECHESIS
A New Vision Based on the Liturgy and the Catechism of the Catholic Church

Dominic F. Ashkar

Paper, 192 pages

5" x 8", 0-89390-342-6

Does publication of the Catechism of the Catholic Church signal a move away from liturgical reform? Not in the eyes of Fr. Dominic F. Ashkar. This religious educator says the Catechism springs from the same well as the Liturgy. In fact, they work together to suggest seven principles that can rejuvenate your catechetical program. These principles, derived from the story of the transfiguration, begin with the call of a disciple to ascend a high mountain and end with the sending of the disciple on a journey.

ROAD TO EMMAUS
A New Model for Catechesis

Dominic F. Ashkar

Paper, 200 pages

5" x 8", 0-89390-266-7

Put new life into your teaching. Study, reflect, integrate the ten principles outlined in this book and the results will be evident in your programs and in parish life. Great for catechist training.

EUCHARIST
An Eight-Session Ritual-Catechesis Experience for Adults

Susan S. Jorgensen

Paper, 200 pages

8" x 11", 0-89390-293-4

"Susan Jorgensen has created a living, breathing, working process for community transformation... respectful of differences, open to the variety of approaches. Ready to use and well designed, it is a strong resource and strong spark to our ritual imaginations." - Catholic Press Association Book Award Judges

Participants in this eight-week program work through the prayers of the eucharistic liturgy, from opening rite to dismissal, and emerge with deep understanding of the words and gestures of the Eucharist.

CELEBRATING THE LECTIONARY

Celebrating The Lectionary (CTL) is a Roman Catholic lectionary-based catechetical program for parishes and schools. The program offers teacher packets for six age groups, all coordinated around the same Sunday readings, covering all Sundays from September through June, for an economical price.

The following are the different age groups:

- **Nursery Packet (ages 3-4)**
- **Beginner Packet (ages 4-6)**
- **Primary Packet (ages 7-8)**
- **Intermediate Packet (ages 9-11)**
- **Junior-Senior Packet (ages 11-15)**
- **Adult Packet (ages 15 and up)**

Additional packets provide for Children's Liturgy of the Word, and bilingual Family Handout Masters, Children's Catechumenate, plus support packets for homilists and DREs. Here is what you get in every Catechetical Teacher Packet:

Overview of the Year: The overview shows the lesson themes for each Sunday of the year, and also the themes for the Units that the lessons are grouped into.

Unit Background Sheets: These give background information on the season, the scriptural context of the readings, and the connection between the reading and the related doctrine. They also explain how the theme derives from the readings, and give notes for future preparations that need to be made more than one week in advance.

Sunday Background Sheets: These give commentary on the three readings and the psalm, explaining the historical context, the literary context and the liturgical context of each.

Lesson Plans: Each lesson is divided into the following components: Purpose, Preparation, Opening, Introducing the Theme, Closing. Many include several options for each component.

Activity Sheets: Activity Sheets are handouts that you photocopy and give to each student. They eliminate the need for costly, separate student textbooks.

Resource Sheets: These provide additional material needed in specific lessons. They often include stories, meditations, and craft patterns for the catechist. They are not meant to be handed out.

Teaching Pictures: These are pictures to be shown to the children as you tell a story. Because you paint or color them yourself, you can adapt them to the ethnic makeup of your community.

Catechist's Supplement: This is an additional resource provided with each teaching packet. It contains developmental information, skills for effective catechesis, suggestions for preparation, alternate craft ideas, games, activities, etc.

Order from your local bookseller, or contact:

Resource Publications, Inc.
160 E. Virginia Street #290
San Jose, CA 95112-5876
1-888-273-7782 (voice)
1-408-287-8748 (fax)